Coming up Trumps!

Coming up Trumps!

Four Ways into the Future

DR PETER BRIERLEY

ALL ROYALTIES FROM THIS BOOK WILL GO TOWARDS
FURTHER RESEARCH ON THE CHURCH

10 09 08 07 06 05 04   7 6 5 4 3 2 1

First published 2004 by Authentic Media
9 Holdom Avenue, Bletchley, Milton Keynes, Bucks., MK1 1UQ, UK
and PO Box 1047, Waynesboro, GA 30830–2047, USA
www.authenticmedia.co.uk

British Library Cataloguing in Publication Data
A catalogue record for this book is available from the British Library

ISBN 1–85078–548–1

Cover Design by River
Typeset by Waverley Typesetters, Galashiels
Print Management by Adare Carwin
Printed and Bound in Denmark by Nørhaven Paperback

Dedication

While a book on strategic thinking may not be easy to write, please, reader, do not think this is a process of self-actualisation. It has been honed from dozens of interactions with friends and colleagues down the years, some for a few hours, most for many years, to whom I am eternally grateful for their encouragement, their example, and their enabling me to understand more about things I saw but dimly.

Especially these are: Valerie Akhurst, Rosemary Aldis, Doug Balfour, George Barna, John Boreham, Pete Broadbent, John Brown, Clive Calver, Richard Dannatt, Michael Dare, Nat Davies, Stanley Davies, Ed Dayton, Joel Edwards, Graham Fairbairn, Eddie Gibbs, John Griffiths, Tom Houston, Manfred Kohl, Michael Lawson, David Longley, Fergus McDonald, Ernest Oliver, Chris Radley, Paul Sandham, Colin Saunders, Leith Samuel, Ulla Tervo, Michael Turnbull, James Tysoe, John Wallis, Heather Wraight and Chris Wright.

To all these, together with my four children, who have taught me more about strategic thinking than they will ever know:

STEPHEN, TIMOTHY, KIM AND MICHAEL,

I gratefully dedicate this volume.

Contents

Foreword

Today's Church is dying of short-termism. Faced with declining attendances, lack of money, huge building maintenance costs and a bureaucracy that we neither need nor can afford, bishops and other church leaders make managerial decisions that will tweak the future, but which will ultimately prove to be, in the words of Peter Senge, 'fixes that fail'.[1]

As Senge puts it: 'A fix, effective in the short term, has unforeseen long-term consequences which may require even more use of the same fix ... "It always seemed to work before; why isn't it working now?"'[2]

Peter Brierley has become a good friend over the years as we have argued, puzzled over and worried at this simple conundrum; why it is so rare for those who lead the Church to think and plan in a long-term, visionary and strategic way? Part of the answer is probably the allergy that many clergy and church leaders have towards insights from leadership and management practice. The complaint I hear runs something like this: 'I was called to

---

[1] Peter Senge, *The Fifth Discipline* (Random House, 1990), pp. 388–389.

[2] Ibid, p. 388.

be a priest/pastor/minister of the gospel, not to embrace business techniques.' There's also more than a suspicion that some of the techniques that the Church does embrace are already out of date in the world of industry and commerce!

But I remain convinced that there is no inherent con-tradiction between being a church leader, committed to Jesus Christ and the values of the Kingdom of God, and being a person of vision and leadership, borrowing insights from management disciplines. What is more, it's my belief that the Church needs strategic thinkers. People who can understand the present, reading the signs of the times. People who can see the possibilities of the future, and envisage a number of possible scenarios. Most of all, people who can lead, inspire and help others to see God's future, and lead the Church into that future, full of faith and hope.

Peter believes passionately that we need strategic thinkers and leaders. This book represents his attempt to pass on some of his accumulated wisdom and skill which those who have benefited from his work with Christian Research will readily acknowledge. It's the kind of book you'll want to come back to. Using the metaphor of the card game, you'll want to nominate different trump suits for playing different hands. My hope and prayer is that the book will help many Christian leaders play the long game – and play to win for God!

PETE BROADBENT
Bishop of Willesden

Introduction

As far back as I can remember, I was always keen on numbers, and adept with them. One year at school we had geometry the period before the mid-morning break, in which homework was set, meant to take 30 minutes. Straight to the tuck-shop, where there was table space to work at – our self-designated assignment, could we solve the problems in ten minutes? If not, homework was going to be really hard that week! One evening, walking with my wife-to-be, we passed a leaf-covered garden, so I turned to her and asked in all seriousness, 'How many leaves do you think there are in that garden?' She still married me! Even now when I see a flock of birds in the sky I automatically try to count them.

Such an attitude undoubtedly came from my father, who before the First World War had specialised in Euclid, the father of modern geometry. My fascination was honed by a Polish maths teacher, Bruno Paszylk, who when coaching me for my eleven-plus exam always spent half the time every week in mental arithmetic. Especially, however, it was fed by a brilliant and first-class maths teacher (he had obtained a first at Cambridge in 1928) at school, George Higgins, whose ability and agility with numbers was a total inspiration. So when out for cycle rides in my teens I would be rote learning all the squares ($13^2 = 169$; $16^2 = 256$; $23^2 = 529$; $38^2 = 1,444$, etc.), which are so useful for quick calculations!

However, at university it was suggested I study statistics, not mathematics, a decision for which I am profoundly grateful in retrospect. At University College London we were taught theory in the morning and then spent every afternoon working out what the numbers meant on little calculators where you had to turn the handle round very fast. In this way I learned to compare numbers and assess their meaning.

Converted in my late teens in the last year at school, there was no obvious way of directly combining my Christian faith and my love of numbers, so I began as a religious education teacher, then became a maths teacher. I soon discovered I didn't have the patience to be a good teacher. To me simultaneous equations are so obvious that when one poor lad said, 'Sir, I don't understand, please show me another way,' and I couldn't, I knew teaching was not for me.

Then came eleven enjoyable years in the Civil Service among which for three years we undertook surveys amongst the Armed Forces, and for four-and-a-half years I headed up the new Survey Control Unit in the Central Statistics Office, still part then of the Cabinet Office. Having had the privilege of several positions of responsibility in the churches we attended, I was ready in my late 30s for leadership at work, and was appointed Programme Director of the British and Foreign Bible Society, when Tom Houston was Executive Director.

That was the period when the first English Church Census was undertaken (all analysed by hand!) in 1979, when we started doing multiple research projects, and I stopped producing parts of what is now the *UK*

Christian Handbook in my spare time and produced the first integrated version. It so happened Tom was Chair of the new World Vision of Europe, which followed its American parent by having a MARC component as part of its ministry (MARC stood for Mission Advanced Research and Communication Centre). I was asked to set up MARC Europe with the brief 'to strengthen Christian leadership in Europe'.

It was a most wonderful and challenging opportunity. We discovered that many church leaders had little management training and with the help of a brilliant ex-Head of Training at Shell, Dr David Cormack, we began a huge programme of leadership seminars, a hundred a year at their peak. One was on Vision Building. David said to me that I couldn't help him with it until first I knew my own vision. That was a deep challenge, which took me nine months to work out into a formulary in which I could merge my love for the Lord and for numbers: 'he counted for God'. I would love that phrase for my epitaph, unworthy though I have been in its fulfilment.

In 1988, David Wavre, then of Hodder & Stoughton, asked me to write a book: *Vision Building.* That was a tough undertaking! But it opened up a ministry of interacting with dozens of churches and Christian organisations, who asked me to facilitate their thinking in this area. This has been and still is a huge privilege. Meanwhile, research assignments continued to come, some major, many minor. Over the 1990s, however, apart from changing our name to Christian Research, we were also beginning to be asked not just to explain the research findings in a debrief with the sponsoring agency, but to say what they meant for the organisation or church concerned.

Thinking about interpretation and application of research, trying to understand the 'big picture' (lots of church statistics were included in the UK Christian Handbook's companion publication *Religious Trends*) and repeatedly being asked 'So what?' led me to continue to think how to work our way into the future. At a missions conference one weekend in Connecticut, United States, I heard about Horizon Mission Methodology. Following it up excitedly, I began to use it when asked to undertake Vision Building days. That's how I learned the pragmatics of this, very different, approach.

I describe in Chapter 6 how I learned about Relating and Delegating during my visit to South Africa in 2001, and in Chapter 7 about the guts of the Military Model in 2002, although elements of both had been incorporated in my time management seminar, which I undertake twice a year under the title 'Priorities, Planning and Paperwork'.

These came at a time when I was desperately concerned about the need to think strategically about the church in this country. The third English Church Census, undertaken in 1998, the results of which were published in *The Tide is Running Out* in 2000, worried me deeply. We were losing so many children! Help! What *was* the church to do? We started a small Strategic Think-Tank that met over 18 months and an annual Strategic Thinkers' Forum, both of which have helped me enormously to try and wrestle with the issue of strategic thinking, and beyond that to strategic action. I am hugely indebted to those who joined in those many discussions, not just in their substance, but in the methodology used. Looking back now on the long chats I had with my mother during weekly visits to her in the 1980s and 1990s – she lived nearby till her death in 2001 – I realise that she was clearly a strategic thinker.

Thus did a statistician used to analysing research projects get motivated to work out what the results might mean and then to apply that kind of explanatory mechanism to much wider tasks involving the church as a whole. My understanding of my own projections worry me; I don't like what I see and long to do something about it. Internally at Christian Research we say that our vision is to do all we can to make sure that the trends we forecast don't come true!

Perhaps this little volume will be a contribution towards the work that has to be done in changing the culture of the church. Joseph told Pharaoh that his seven good years would be followed by seven poor ones. The number seven may not be appropriate, but I do believe we have only a short window of opportunity for the church and the Christian faith before dark times come. The night comes when no one can work, said Jesus. Let us therefore do everything we can while it is still day! And may the Lord bless you in your working it out!

Dr Peter Brierley
Executive Director
Christian Research
January 2004

Chapter 1

What is Strategic Thinking?

His vision was very clear. Five-year-old Jimmie was sent off to bed one evening by his parents. To their surprise when they came to check that all was well an hour or so later they found him not in bed but staring out of the window.

'What are you doing?' they asked.

'Looking at the moon,' he replied. 'One day I'm going to walk on it.' And, 32 years later, James Irwin did just that! He is one of the 12 human beings who have had that privilege so far.

But having the vision did not automatically mean that it would be fulfilled. James determined to study the right subjects at school and to do them well, to graduate with an appropriate degree from university and to take a relevant job when he began to work. When NASA was choosing who should be on the Apollo flights, they didn't just make a list of the 250 million people in the United States and use the proverbial pin to select who might go. Not at all: they carefully scrutinised a long list of possible candidates picked for their experience, qualifications and character. James Irwin had to be on that list and to stand out as having the right abilities in order to have a chance of selection.

Translating his childhood vision into reality required clear strategic thinking – itself one of the reasons why he was probably chosen. He knew what he wanted to do and made certain he was equipped as far as he humanly could be. So it was with gritty determination that he fought back to fitness after a nearly fatal motorbike accident, which broke almost every bone in his body. His vision translated into specific action time and again.

Building extension

The new minister, Michael, accepted the vision of the Church Council passed just before he came to the church – that if the church was to grow it needed to be physically extended. It had long since reached the '80% full' mark, which has been shown to inhibit growth in churches (newcomers find either nowhere to sit or only seats at the front, which they dislike).

He also realised, however, that a major constraint to growth was not the limitations of the building (real though these were) but the leadership structure within the church. As later studies have come to show,[1] the smaller the team, the more effective the decision-making process. Michael therefore began to build a strategic group of people who would form his staff team. He abolished the Eldership and began to use the Church Council as a body to discuss policy, but not for making day-to-day operational decisions. Such changes were not welcomed by everyone – 'That's the fifty-sixth change he's introduced since he came six months ago,' one lady observed!

If, however, the vision was to be fulfilled it was essential to have a flexible leadership structure. If structure impacts the running of an organisation, and it doesn't always, then it usually impacts it in a major way. That was the case in this south London church. In order to fulfil a wider agreed objective (growth) the mechanisms by which it could be accomplished had to be put in place. That is strategic thinking. So an administrator was added to the team and, in due course, a youth worker and second curate, as well as a music director.

More had to happen to make the vision of a church extension come to pass, however. Plans had to be drawn up, agreement with church and local authorities reached, finances raised, and the congregation and local community kept informed. This was the detail, highly important, attached to one huge component of the overall strategy.

In addition, a larger congregation has greater pastoral needs. So it became urgent to set up an alternative and efficient pastoral system. Working through the various house groups proved less effective than having a person on the leadership team dedicated to providing, through a small group of trained helpers, rapid and good pastoral advice and support. Michael was only brought in to help with the especially demanding cases, often involving marital disharmony or breakdown.

The church also believed overseas mission was important. Various mission directors were appointed (who were not part of the regular leadership team) who were broadly allowed to exercise their responsibility in line with their own imagination and gifting, checking with Michael on a regular basis so that things outside the overall vision were not diverting resources and energy.

Involvement within the community was essential. A group began helping refugees both with practical issues and arranging language classes. A senior citizens' coffee morning became a thriving a hundred-a-week luncheon club, begun by two dedicated ladies and supported by an inner and extended group of committed helpers.

As a consequence of such careful strategic planning and much patience in getting the necessary permissions for the building and raising the money, the vision took shape, was fulfilled and the extension was built. The new building was by that time much needed because of the growth of the congregation – the *real* vision was also being fulfilled.

Aerial demolished

Going to the moon was not the only innovative project in the 1960s. A Surrey businessman concerned about Gospel needs in India began to challenge church people to do something then thought spectacular – build a huge radio transmitter on the Seychelles Islands off the east coast of Africa, from which radio broadcasts could be made. It was a visionary project that captured the imagination of many, an array of huge masts being built and in use by 1970.

The next 30 years saw these masts do their job brilliantly, reaching some 40 countries in Africa and the Middle East as well as India with regular broadcasts. It became a hallmark of what is now called FEBA Radio.[2] The vision: to reach people with the Good News of Jesus Christ. The means: the masts in the Seychelles. However, in that period of time technology radically changed, and new leadership had to consider the most effective and efficient means of continuing the unchanged vision of reaching men and women for Christ by means of radio.

Can the vision stay the same but the means of achieving it be radically altered? After careful discussion over two years at the beginning of the 21st century, the Board and senior staff produced a new strategic plan, with better, mostly more local, ways of reaching the same audiences. This included demolishing the mast and leaving the Seychelles.

The Surrey businessman, now in his 80s, was still committed to the cause underlying the reason for the mast in the first place, and was agreeable to the decision made – to terminate broadcasts from the Seychelles on

31st March 2003. Not many people have the courage to 'watch the things you gave your life to, broken / And stoop and build 'em up with worn-out tools',[3] although, to be fair, the revitalisation of the work of FEBA was hardly with worn-out tools, but rather with the new tools of up-to-date technologies. It was still not an easy decision for him, however, and the price of renewed vision is sometimes the literal demolition of the past. Strategic evaluation can require total renewal, not partial redevelopment.

Strategic thinking

A *definition*

These three examples of vision required more than grandiose ideas of the future. They demanded careful and detailed work to ensure that the desired end was accomplished. That kind of planning is an integral part of what is called in this book 'strategic thinking'. How may strategic thinking be defined? Here is one working definition:

> Strategic thinking is the ability to think and plan with long-term insight, in the light of current developments, and to identify consequent deliverable key areas of action.

This statement has a number of elements, which will be taken clause by clause. It is not only about 'thinking'!

think and plan . . .
The ability to envision the future is highly important and crucial to the whole process. Strategic thinking has to progress beyond seeing what has to happen to working through specifically how it could be achieved. 'Planning'

is a process requiring careful thought, but it can also be spoken about rationally, argued for where necessary, and is capable of being committed to writing. If you like, 'thinking' is the conception and development; 'planning' is the delivery and the opportunity for fulfilment.

with long-term insight . . .
How long is 'long term' will vary with the project in question. If a mayfly could think and realise its average life was just three hours, long term might be a hundred minutes! Constructing and using a new building might require three or five years. Wanting to see a congregation double in size might mean a five- or ten-year plan. For oil companies like Shell, which have to seek out reservoirs of oil for future use, 30 years may be typical. The importance here is less the length of time involved, more the ability to think future, to think forwards, to think ahead. Not everyone can.

The phrase, however, actually involves more than the ability to think just about what is to come. In the early months of 2003 many realised it was only a matter of time before America declared war on Iraq. In a sense, that was thinking future. The above phrase, however, includes the word 'insight' – what would be the implications of an American invasion? An American victory? A subsequent American administration? Answering those kinds of questions is much more difficult, as the immediate aftermath of the war demonstrated.

I was once shown a detailed five-year strategy by an important, international and large organisation. It was an interesting document with a huge number of details as to how each segment of the work would be accomplished year by year and country by country. Nowhere, however, was it stated *why* the work was to be done; there was no vision statement and no sense of insight as to the consequences of the tasks it was proposing.

Long-term insight is thus the ability to *understand the impact* of the changes being proposed or actions being considered and, when necessary, to take action in advance to forestall any undesirable implications they may have. It is the ability to envisage what the world will be like if it changes as anticipated and living, as it were, in the reality of that new world.

in the light of current developments . . .

Futuristic speculation is not strategic thinking. Science fiction is an enjoyable genre of writing, the best of which subtly devolves from where the world is currently placed. It is fun, but by and large only of enjoyment value. For a vision to be of any value it needs to be earthed in present reality. Daniel's visions of the future kingdoms started with the one he was already in; Nebuchadnezzar's huge statue included Nebuchadnezzar himself as the head.

What is happening at the moment? What are the implications? Noting some of the major current cultural elements can be helpful for beginning the task of working through their consequences. That is why the next chapter seeks to set out some of the factors of the current UK church scene, both as a way of helping strategic thinking and also to illustrate the actual process.

So strategic thinkers have to be able to evaluate the present as well as anticipate the future.

to identify . . . action

It is critical that a strategic thinker can deliver actionable steps towards his/her goal. If you are going to cross the river you need to be able to say where the stepping stones are. At the initial stage it may not be possible to know how many stepping stones there may be, or in what shape they may come, but it is essential to know that they will be there.

Strategic thinking, however, is not confined to ascertaining where the stepping stones should be. It is also determining whether or not crossing the river is best done by way of stepping stones, or whether it would be better to use the bridge or the ferry – or indeed if one should attempt to cross this river at all.

Action in this context is not indiscriminate, doing something as the mood takes you. This is a careful, deliberate act of the will along a chosen path designed to achieve the desired object. It is not the use of surplus energy or finding ways to keep the young people occupied. It is knowing what has to be accomplished by when and going for it.

consequent deliverable key areas of action

The action that has to be planned has two further characteristics in addition to aiming towards the desired target. The actions have to be logical, derived from the vision or ultimate aim to be achieved. This demands more than just working out what has to be done. Actions need to be put into some kind of priority, based on factors such as how difficult they are to accomplish, the resources available to complete them, and the time within which ideally they should be finished.

These actions have to be 'deliverable', that is, achievable and specific. There will come a period in the implementation process by which a person will know whether or not they have been achieved. In other words, they are measurable in some specified way. It is moving from the general 'growing our congregation' to the specific 'seeing it double in size in five years'. There is also the implied need for the actions to be reasonable and realistic. There is no point saying you aim to climb Everest if the resources available to you mean at best you could get to the top of Snowdon!

Finally, there is deliberately one more important word in the definition of strategic thinking – 'key' areas of action. This implies that the strategic thinker has the ability to weigh up the various possibilities and choose those which are most critical. The most important paths are not always chosen, but putting time and energy on the less important (not necessarily the wrong) paths is actually a waste of time in the long term. People have to have confidence in their leader that he/she is able to choose the right priorities amidst the babble of suggestions that may be made. It is not a question of doing *anything* to meet the demands of the day, but rather choosing the best options for the future, even if it takes longer to make that choice and begin the process in the first place.

This has implications for the strategic thinker personally. He/she needs a steady nerve, the ability not to be swayed by the forces of the moment, calmness in thought, and an unswerving commitment to the ultimate purpose. Such are rightly named Captains of Industry, and they can be recognised as Captains of the Church also, even if that title is not altogether appropriate! Those who work with such need to follow their example and to learn as much as they can from them. I suspect that might mean that good strategic thinkers are avid readers of biographies!

A shorter definition

If the above discussion seems like a sledgehammer to crack a nut, here is a simpler and shorter definition. Meeting a former colleague, Dr Bryant Myers, a Vice-President with

World Vision International, at the funeral of a mutual friend,[4] and knowing that he was a strategist *par excellence*, I asked him point blank for a definition of a strategic thinker. He replied with only a moment's hesitation:

· Looking at the trends and taking appropriate leverage action.

If that fits easier for you, use that instead!

The parameters of strategic thought

The 1960s educational reformer Piaget once defined operational thinking as 'The ability to reason in the abstract without having to rely on concrete objects or events'[5] and went on to say that he thought only about 30% of adults could do this. In another study, researchers Birch and Malim found that 'operational thought is found in our culture only among 30–40% of adults'.[6] This may explain why thinking is not a popular subject – *Teach Yourself to Think* was published in the 1940s[7] but has been out of print since!

It may be argued that operational thought and strategic thought are not the same. Maybe they are not, but the limitations of one are probably likely to apply to the other. In other words, this is suggesting that perhaps a third of adults might be able to think strategically. Are church leaders typical in this respect? Even if they are, it must be strongly stated that this does not imply that the other two-thirds cannot think (!) nor that they cannot lead! It simply suggests that they think and lead in other ways.

Paul makes it clear that Christian people have different gifts and encourages us to use the gifts we have been given to the full. In that process we may come across one or two gifts we didn't know we had! In describing the gift of strategic thinking I am hoping to help those with the gift to use it better, and to help some to recognise that they have it. There is absolutely no criticism implied about those who find this topic is of no interest to them.

The *ability* to think strategically is not, however, the only constricting parameter. There are others. Professor John Adair, an international consultant in the field of leadership, well known for teaching management principles in the 1970s and 1980s in the UK and who in retirement was appointed to advise the Church of England's Archbishops' Council, said there were three components to any job: the nature of the actual task to be done; the team through whom it was to be accomplished; and the characteristics of the individual who was going to do the job.

All three are important with respect to strategic thinking because they help to identify which of the various methods, outlined in Chapters 4 to 7, of such thinking would be applicable for a particular person or in particular circumstances. We will look at each of these three one by one.

The task to be done

Leaders have different responsibilities, and that is as true of church leaders as of any others. The diagram on page 12[8] illustrates how the nature of leadership responsibility varies by the size of a church's congregation. Similar diagrams could be drawn with respect to any leadership position as the work gets larger or more complex; the nature of the diagram will not alter in broad outline although the title of the bottom axis will.

Figure 1.1
The increasing complexity of congregational leadership

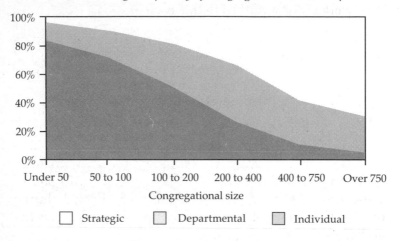

This diagram may be read as follows:

- All church leaders have to engage with individual members of their congregation; in smaller churches where there is little intermediate leadership, most of that interaction, and especially guidance for work to be undertaken, will come from direct face-to-face involvement by the minister. As the size of the church increases, some of the communication will be done by the minister through intermediaries. In a business these might be called 'departmental heads', but in a church are called 'Warden', 'Chief Steward', 'Youth Leader', 'Deacon', 'Elder', 'Administrator', etc. In the largest churches nearly all communication will be through such people.

- As a church increases in size the need to appoint 'departmental heads' will increase accordingly, whether these are part time or full time, paid or voluntary, ordained or non-ordained.

- There is always a need to think carefully ahead, but as the church increases in size the senior minister will be required to spend more time in such strategic planning and discussions. In the largest churches much of the key work is accomplished in this way.

There is one other element in the diagram that is important. The demands of strategic thinking do not increase linearly with responsibility. At some stage there is a 'mega' jump, which tentatively I have suggested occurs at the 400 to 750 mark, meaning that the dynamic leadership of a church of 400 or more requires different kinds of abilities to those leading smaller churches. Many ministers leading churches of, say, 200 can, with help, move to lead a church of 250. But not every minister of a church of 300 is capable of effectively leading a church of, say, 400, even with help. The difference, in part, is the ability to think strategically.

I have seen this personally in a church I know well. A committed minister came to a church of about 250 in the mid–1970s and faithfully preached and led the church for a number of years. The Lord blessed his ministry and the church grew to about 400. The minister found himself under increasing strain and tried to find alternative methods of oversight, but ultimately realised the job was too big for him. He therefore left and went to pastor a congregation of 200, which he did very satisfactorily until he retired, again seeing growth to about 250. His replacement in the original church was a man who was used to large congregations and quickly made the necessary adjustments to allow the church to flourish. No criticism is implied of the minister who moved; he and his successor simply had different leadership gifts, one of which was the ability to think strategically.

Some years ago in a seminar held in Britain, Eddie Gibbs, now Professor of Church Growth at Fuller Theological Seminary, Los Angeles, put this another way:

- The management style of a minister of a church of under fifty people is akin to that of a foreman or supervisor who delegates but retains decision responsibility. There is therefore a high dependency on the minister by the church.

- When the church is between 50 and 200 the management style is closer to that of junior management in a company where there is some delegation but the church still revolves around the one full-time person, who has to act as a multi-talented generalist.

- Between 200 and 350, the style is that of middle management with clear delegation of authority, and the leader's role being much more to provide support for those working at the coalface.

- Between 350 and 600, the style reflects that of senior management with a growing ministry team consisting of full-time professionals rather than part-time volunteers.

- Over 600, the minister acts like the Chair of the Board in a highly complex management structure, giving clear strategic directions.

This also reflects the work of David Wasdell, who in a paper 30 years ago[9] showed that churches had one full-time person for the first 150 or 200 people and then had a further full-time person for every subsequent 150 or part-150 people. In more recent years, churches have often added more paid staff (usually full time) than the 'one per 150' formula, as the ministry demands have increased and people in the church are often more willing to give their money than their time for demanding (and professional) assignments.

The team to work with

An analysis of the way that different generations work shows that there is an increasing recognition of the importance of teams and their composition. Older people tended to focus more on the job to be done rather than the people doing it,[10] whereas 'Boomers' (those in their 40s and 50s) want to be sure the job uses their particular gifting. Generation X (currently those in their 20s and 30s) tend, however, to look at the people they will be working with rather more than the actual job to be done. People and relationships matter hugely to them. Much has been written about the differences today between Generation Xers, Boomers and Builders (in their 60s and early 70s).[11]

The style of leadership varies with the type of team with whom the leader is working. Here are some:[12]

- Some teams *depend* on their leader. This is often true in smaller churches, but is also related to the specialist nature of the work (and the professional skills of the leader), and the experience and qualifications of those in the team. In such teams the leader is crucial and his/her thinking prescribes the outcome of the job being done.

- Some teams work well because there is a joint interest in the *outcome*. The story is told[13] of a 12th-century Lord of the Manor visiting a cathedral under construction. 'What are you doing?' he asked one stonemason. 'I'm shaping this stone to go into that pillar,' he replied. 'And what are you doing?' he asked another. 'I'm helping to build a cathedral,' that mason replied. Despite much labour unrest at the time, when Coventry Cathedral was being built in the late 1950s and early 1960s no strike took place among the workforce: 'We may never have the chance to build another cathedral,' workers said. The leader here is simply the holder of the vision.

- The *skills* in a team will sometimes determine the style of leadership. A good leader will mentor, or guide, those with whom he/she is working and encourage them to become more proficient in the way they do their part of the job. The leader here is more like a teacher.

- The *expectation* of a team can be all important. In a Southampton school some years ago one of the maths teachers was known to be especially strict and made his pupils work very hard.[14] Those who were selected for his set, however, usually rejoiced. 'We *know* we are going to pass maths now,' they would say. Some people *want* to work with a particular leader because of his past reputation. The leader here acts as a kind of guru, an example to be followed.

This is looking at the task to be done from the viewpoint of the team member. The leader, however, will vary his/her approach according to the perception he/she has of the team – what are the members' values? Their inclination to get on with the job? How much confidence do the members have in themselves? How mature are the members in working together?

The leader also has to take into account the actual work to be undertaken. How many people are needed? What are the requirements of this particular piece of work? How quickly has this got to be completed? Has this been attempted before, and, if so, with what results?

One of the findings of the 2002 Scottish Church Census[15] was that the *size* of a team was important *vis-à-vis* church growth. Growing churches had an average lay leadership of 13 people, churches stable over the previous eight years had an average team of 19 people and declining churches a team of 22 people. The smaller the leadership team, the more effective it proved to be. A smaller number of people, willing to take risks, able to think strategically ahead and to identify the vision was better than a larger group with other, wider gifts.

The individuals in the team

The third component relates to the abilities of the individual people who comprise the team and who together will lead the church, the project or whatever. What gifts do they bring to the task? There are a number of personality tests like Myers-Briggs[16] or Le Haye, motivational tests like McClelland,[17] or transactional analysis[18] to help people learn how they communicate with others. By way of example we will focus just on one, which a number of organisations, including Christian Research, have used for many years, and which hundreds of church leaders have found helpful – the Belbin Test.[19]

Meredith Belbin was a management consultant at the Henley College of Management for a number of years in the 1970s and also undertook a similar role in a like centre in Australia. It was in these locations that he made his far-reaching observations on the nature of management teams. His key observation was that those working in team situations bring at least one of eight critical skills to that task. Some may bring more than one, and in fact many do. Very few bring six or seven or all eight, however.

He further observed that not all the various combinations of these characteristics actually work to produce successful teams. There are a few combinations that simply don't work

The basic book in which his ideas are worked out is *Management Teams*, published by Butterworth-Heinemann initially in 1981, but it has been reprinted virtually every year since. In his more recent writings he has introduced a ninth 'type', the specialist who functions as a team member on a part-time basis, usually only while his/her particular topic is being discussed at a meeting – such as an architect brought in to a planning meeting that is looking at building an extension to a church.

Meredith Belbin produced a questionnaire that helped to identify which of these eight different characteristics people have.[20] It has been found to be remarkably robust, and consistent over time, over age, for both genders, and over different cultures and ethnic groups. By answering the questions on the Belbin sheet the different characteristics can be ascertained for a particular individual.[21] It is possible to get a sophisticated computer programme that will analyse the results very fully.

One of the disadvantages of Belbin's work is that he uses what seem to be strange names for some of his attributes (the reason for which is explained in *Management Teams*). A more readily understandable description of each is given below!

The eight main characteristics
The following is a brief overview of the eight factors. Essentially they are in four pairs:

The Thinking Axis

- **A** are those with a creative mind, constantly able to think of new ideas, not only in terms of products but also in terms of relationships. Creative people may not necessarily be good 'people-people', but they are often good at thinking how difficult relationships can be resolved.

- **B** are critical people who in many ways are the reverse of the creative and frequently can tell creative people why their ideas will not work. This leads to a natural tension between them, but that tension is not usually destructive.

The Information Axis

- **C** represents the detail people who are excellent at proofreading, making sure minute things are correct, will invariably ensure that the totals on a page of numbers tally, and usually check the small print without being asked.

- **D** are resource people who frequently know where to find something, know where to go to get a certain skill, or know people who do. They are excellent at networking and highly useful in situations where many different types of need may be present. Many clergy are resource people.

The Work Axis

- The Work Axis is divided between those who are **E**, task people, who like to get jobs completed, and **F** people, whose joy is to meet people and share with them. Both are needed in work situations, and help make any church work run more smoothly. Many church volunteers, and probably volunteers generally, are task or team people.

The Leadership Axis

- **G** is the Director or Co-ordinator[22] who operates on the basis of 'How?' and seeks to indicate the ways by which actions can be fulfilled, how a vision can be worked out, the mechanisms that need to be in place in order to ensure that something happens. Often, but not always, the Director is better with people than a Shaper.

- **H** is the Shaper type who often tends to make things happen either by the force of his/her personality or because of the relevance of the circumstances. The Shaper operates on the principle 'Why?' – what is the reason for this particular action, what is its purpose, what do we hope to achieve by doing this?

- It is these two which when present on a team can bring intolerable strain on relationships because of their different ways of leadership, and some teams break under that strain.

Team dynamics

In a team of a small number of people, say six or less, those present will need to exercise two or more of their particular strengths. Those who are part of a larger team, say sixteen people or more, may well find that there are two or three others present who have a dominant strength similar to theirs.

People with scores on any particular axis that are very close or even identical (which is quite common) have the advantage of being able to understand both points of view, though people will often not know which viewpoint they are representing at any particular moment in time. It can therefore help if in their communication process they can give some indication of which side they are coming from. If, for example, they are equally a creative person and a critic, they might wish to preface some of their comments by saying something like 'That's a good idea, why don't we . . .' or 'I'm not sure I agree with that because . . .' Such phrases subconsciously indicate to everyone else which particular attribute they are about to use.

How church people score

Many have found Meredith Belbin's team leadership structure accurate, relevant and helpful. Some suggest more modern ways of describing leadership are better, but major organisations like the Royal Mail were using Belbin's work very publicly in 2002. Several studies have used his work to identify the type of team input church leaders have. A study amongst 150 Anglican clergy in the Diocese of Bradford in 1995[23] found that 18% of them were either Directors or Shapers. An analysis of 305 members of the Christian Research Association in 1997 found 35% of Anglican clergy could be described in this way, 26% of non-Anglican clergy and 29% of lay people.[24] A survey of 1,125 English ministers undertaken for the Salvation Army in 2002 found that 32% were either Directors or Shapers.[25] The table below summarises these three; the sources for each are given in the notes at the end of the chapter.

Table 1.2
Church and lay leadership and the Belbin Test

Type	Source	Brad D Anglican clergy %	CRA Members Anglican clergy %	CRA Members Other clergy %	CRA Members Lay people %	Salvation Army Study Anglican clergy %	Salvation Army Study Other clergy %	Combined figures Anglican clergy %	Combined figures Other clergy %
A	Creative	11	8	3	9	7	7	7	7
B	Critic	13	14	10	8	11	9	12	9
C	Detail	18	3	13	9	6	8	6	9
D	Resourcer	15	26	21	19	24	18	24	18
E	Task	7	7	14	17	9	12	9	12
F	Team	17	7	13	9	12	13	12	13
G	Director	8	18	13	14	17	19	16	18
H	Shaper	10	17	13	15	14	14	14	14
	Base	42	90	77	138	406	592	538	669

Brad D = Broadford Diocese

This table suggests that Anglican clergy are more likely to be critics and resourcers than other clergy, and that non-Anglican clergy are more likely to be detail and task people. It may be too great a parody, but this suggests that Anglicans know where to go to get something done, non-Anglicans like doing it!

On the assumption that those with clear leadership gifts (which is what Directors and Shapers have) are likely to be strategic thinkers, then these studies support the other findings mentioned earlier that perhaps about a third of adults can think strategically.

One of the parameters of strategic thought, therefore, is that perhaps only about a third of church leaders, as a third of most people, can readily think this way.[26] In a mode or place where strategic thinking becomes critical it is therefore important to try and ensure that those engaged in the exercise actually have the ability to do it!

Leadership and strategic thinking type
The reason for giving all this detail is so that the leader may know (or guess!) the Belbin type(s) he/she is and his/her team members are. Having an understanding of what each member brings to the team situation does, of itself, help in the way tasks are presented, vision is communicated and strategic thinking is undertaken. This is because the fulfilment has to be worked through the gifting of each individual team member.

Different ways of thinking strategically vary according to the Belbin type, as is suggested in Table 1.3, though there are always exceptions:

Table 1.3
Strategic thinking mode by Belbin characteristic

Mode \ Axis	♣ Vision Building	♦ Horizon Mission Methodology	♥ Relating & Delegating	♠ Military Model
Thinking	✓	✓		
Information	✓		✓	✓
Work	✓		✓	
Leadership		✓	✓	✓

Postmodern teams

Of the various demographic factors between people in the 21st century, church people or otherwise, age or the generational factor is probably the most significant. The two later studies reflected in Table 1.2 contained an analysis by age group, and these have been added together to give the numbers in Table 1.4:

Table 1.4
Belbin characteristics by age group

Type	Age	Under 40s %	40s %	50s %	60s & over %
A	Creative	7	10	4	4
B	Critic	10	13	9	8
C	Detail	6	4	8	10
D	Resourcer	24	24	24	18
E	Task	12	11	10	15
F	Team	11	8	15	18
G	Director	10	15	18	16
H	Shaper	20	15	12	11
	Base	136	448	492	352

In turn, these suggest the types of strategic thinking that may be most closely associated with particular age groups, shown in Table 1.5:

Table 1.5
Strategic thinking mode by age group

Axis	Mode	♣ Vision Building	♦ Horizon Mission Methodology	♥ Relating & Delegating	♠ Military Model
Gen Xers		✓	✓	✓	✓
Boomers		✓	✓	✓	
Builders		✓			✓

This chapter has defined strategic thinking and how different ways of implementing it will change according to the circumstances that an individual leader faces and the characteristics of his/her team. Tom Bentley, the Director of the think-tank Demos, gave the results of survey undertaken at a seminar:[27] respondents said the key feature of what makes a 'good leader' was the ability to think strategically. So this is not an optional extra.

In the Glasgow Science Centre there is one exhibit that tells you 'how to think'. It says: Ask questions, draw, write, think laterally, think metaphorically, make checklists, reverse the problem, create storyboards. All these are doubtless important and useful. This book is not about thinking, however – it is strictly about *strategic* thinking. There is a difference! A survey of the top ten business schools in the United States showed their graduates especially excelled in *strategic* thinking.[28]

Before looking specifically at the different ways of strategic thinking mentioned, we need first to look at the context in which such must be placed and then some examples of the ways the different methods have been used in Scripture.

Notes

[1]   As in Peter Brierley, *Turning the Tide: The Challenge Ahead – The Results of the 2002 Scottish Church Census* (Edinburgh: Church of Scotland, and London: Christian Research, 2003), which proved that growing churches have the smallest leadership teams.

[2]   FEBA originally stood for Far East Broadcasting Association.

[3]   'If' by Rudyard Kipling, from *A Choice of Kipling's Verse*, made by T.S. Eliot (London: Faber, 1961).

[4] That of Ed Dayton, on 25th January 2001 in Los Angeles, California.

[5] Quoted in A. Birch and T. Malim, *Developmental Psychology from Infancy to Adulthood* (Intertext, Bristol, 1988), p. 33, but taken from G.F. Kimber's thesis *An Investigation into the Attitude of a Warwickshire Mining Community to Church and Spirituality* (University of Birmingham, February 2001), pp. 58, 59.

[6] Birch and Malim, *Developmental Psychology*, p. 103.

[7] *The Bookseller*, 7th March 2003, p. 26.

[8] This diagram is not based on specific research but is purely illustrative of the points being made.

[9] Revd David Wasdell, *Towards a Parish Strategy* (London: Urban Church Project, June 1975).

[10] This analysis has appeared in several publications. In summary it is given in Brierley, *Turning the Tide*, Table 4.10, p. 58.

[11] See, for example, a comprehensive survey in Peter Brierley, *Reaching and Keeping Tweenagers* (London: Christian Research, 2003), ch. 1.

[12] These factors came from seminars conducted by Dr David Cormack, 'Making the Most of Your Team', by MARC Europe, London in the 1980s in the UK.

[13] This story originally came from Anne Townsend's book *Mid-life Crisis* (Bath: Creative, 1987).

[14] Based on actual personal experience in Deanery Secondary School, Southampton, 1965, watching the teacher concerned and hearing what the children said.

[15] Brierley, *Turning the Tide*, p. 91.

[16] See, for example, Isabel Briggs Myers, *An Introduction to Type* (Oxford Psychologists Press, 1994), or Jenny Rogers, *Sixteen Personality Types* (London: Management Futures, 1997).

[17] Article by D.H. McClelland, 'Power the Inner Experience', *Harvard Business Review, 1976*, and related work with D. Berlew of McBer & Co, Boston, United States.

[18] Such as *Putting People First* (Time Management International, Solihull, 1992, but published by Scandinavian Service School, 1983).

[19] See R. Meredith Belbin's book, *Management Teams: Why they Succeed or Fail* (London: Butterworth-Heinemann, originally published in 1981 but very frequently reprinted).

[20] Any reader interested in completing such a form may obtain one from Christian Research, whose address is given on page 219.

[21] Each person completing the form scores between 0 and 14 points for each. The person with 14 for a particular attribute is not necessarily twice as good as somebody with a score of seven for the same attribute, since we all score ourselves with differing degrees of strength. It is therefore not so much the magnitude of the score allocated but the one(s) that are highest. It is also important to look at the differences between the scores and observe where the gaps between scores are greatest. The attributes where scores are higher than the largest difference will be the ones that tend to represent a person best. Suppose, for example, someone had scored a 14, 13, 12 and 9 for their highest four attributes. The first three differ by only one point but there is a difference of three points between the third and the fourth. The first three represent the person's main attributes, and the fourth could be discounted.

[22] Belbin describes this as 'Chairman', but this word carries unintended connotations, so the word 'Director' is used instead.

[23] Revd Canon Rod Anderson, 'Overgreat Expectations', *Quadrant*, Bulletin of Christian Research, January 1996, p. 6.

[24] 'Leaders and their Team Roles', *Quadrant*, Bulletin of Christian Research, January 1998, p. 1, also analyses the figures by gender and age group. They were based on 305 members of the Christian Research Association.

[25] Based on the analysis of a detailed survey of 1,125 ministers about church growth on behalf of the Salvation Army, in a private research report, *Growing Churches: Why do they Grow?*, July 2002, the broad results of which were published in *Leadership, Vision and Growing Churches* (Manchester: Salvation Army, and London: Christian Research, 2003).

[26] It should be noted that this is much larger than a poll in the United States where only 5% of 601 pastors identified leadership as their primary gift, although the wording here is quite different from that used for the Belbin results (Eddie Gibbs and Ian Coffey, *ChurchNext* [Nottingham: IVP, 2001]).

[27] Seminar 'Leadership: The Challenge for All?' co-ordinated by the Strategic Planning Society, the Chartered Management Institute, Demos, Department for Education and Skills and the Council for Excellence in Management and Leadership on 24th October 2002.

[28] *Trend Letter*, Vol. 20, No. 18, 10th September 2001, p. 7.

Chapter 2

The Context of Vision

Auguste Rodin's statue[1] *The Thinker* captures brilliantly a man deep in thought, pondering difficult things in an unhurried manner, struggling to understand the world about him. The statue shows this kind of thinking to be hard, dedicated work, taking much time to be effective, and requiring concentration in a unique way. Rodin clearly knew what strategic thinking meant!

The Microsoft Business Solutions advertisement[2] was clear: 'Questions are everywhere,' it said. 'Insight is not.' The small print went on to say that helping you to make smarter decisions was their business and they had the resources to help you succeed.

When she was the senior leader of Gallup in the UK, Mrs Jill Garrett, in a seminar[3] for chief executives, said that successful leaders ask themselves questions that unsuccessful ones do not. One of these was 'What does the future look like?'

While Chapter 8 looks at the importance of strategic leadership, in this chapter we are going to try and answer this question with respect to the church, mainly in the UK, though the first item looks world-wide. We are not scrutinising the impact of society on the church, important though that is, since this is covered elsewhere,[4] but at the church itself.

Church growth world-wide

What happens in the world at large has to have some significance for every country around the globe. One of the things that is happening is an increasing urbanisation, with the phrase 'the global village' becoming more properly 'the global city', as 49% of the world's population lived in urban areas in 2003,[5] up from 37% in 1970. Another is the world-wide growth of the church, a key component for every church or Christian agency leader.

According to the editor of the *World Christian Encyclopedia*, Dr David Barrett, there were 2.1 billion Christians on Planet Earth in 2003, 33.1% of the population. This number is rising: the Christian community was 1.8 billion in 1990 (when the percentage was 33.2% of the world's population), 1.9 billion in 1995 and 2 billion in 2000. Over the 13 years 1990 to 2003 the Christian community has grown by 0.3 billion people, or an average of 69,300 people per day.

By comparison the world's population, which stood at 5.3 billion in 1990 and 6.3 billion in 2003, has been growing at the rate of 213,100 per day, so that a third, 32.5%, of the world's increase is Christian. The fact that 32.5% is slightly smaller than the percentage of Christians in the world, 33.1%, indicates that the *rate* of Christian increase is marginally less than sufficient to maintain the status quo. David Barrett, however, forecasts an *increase* in the Christian proportion to 33.4% by 2025.

While it is therefore true that the church is growing world-wide, it is doing so primarily because the population of the world is increasing, and not because the church is gaining more than might naturally be expected. This statement applies to the global picture, but when that picture is broken down by continent, an important variant on the story emerges. The salient figures are given in Table 2.1:

Coming up Trumps!

Table 2.1
Christians by continent, 1990 and 2003

Continent	1990			2003			1990–2003		
	A:Pop	C:Cn	P:%Cn	A:Pop	C:Cn	P:%Cn	D:Pop+	E:Cn+	F:%Cn+
Africa	614	277	45	837	386	46	47,000	23,000	49
Asia	3,182	249	8	3,825	333	9	135,100	17,700	13
Europe	722	550	76	729	561	77	1,500	2,300	153
Latin America	440	409	93	540	504	93	21,100	19,900	94
Northern America	282	240	85	317	267	84	7,400	5,600	76
Oceania	26	22	85	31	26	84	1,000	800	80
WORLD TOTAL	**5,266**	**1,747**	33	**6,279**	**2,077**	33	**213,100**	**69,300**	33

A: Pop = Population of each continent in millions
C: Cn = Christians in each continent in millions
P: %Cn = Percentage of population who are Christian (C as percentage of A)
D: Pop+ = Daily population growth (A:Pop in 2003 less 1990 divided by 13 × 365)
E: Cn+ = Daily Christian growth (C:Cn in 2003 less 1990 divided by 13 × 365)
F: %Cn+ = Population increase who are Christian (E as percentage of D)

This table is interesting. It shows:

- The proportion of the population that is Christian has grown slightly in Africa, Asia and Europe, and remained steady or dropped slightly in Latin America, Northern America and Oceania. Since most of the Christian people counted in 1990 will still be alive and thus counted also in 2003, massive changes would not be expected.

- The proportion of newly born people who are Christian is greater than the general population (showing the church is growing net) in Africa, Asia, Europe and Latin America, although only marginally greater in Latin America.

- The proportion of newly born people who are Christian is much lower in North America and Oceania, especially North America, showing this is the continent where Christianity is, in relative terms, declining most, and that these continents are not passing on the faith to a sufficient proportion of the next generation.

- The high percentage in Europe shows that more people are becoming Christian than are being born, that is, growth is due not only to babies being born into Christian families but also to non-Christian adults turning to Christ. On the face of it, this is excellent news, but the figures are very small, based on many estimates, and are likely to be well within the sampling variations. It must also be remembered that the birth rates in a number of European countries are actually negative (more people die than are born!)

What does all this mean for the UK churches? Although not shown here, it is known that the church has grown significantly across the 20th century in Africa and Asia. The churches in these continents have continued to grow as the 20th century ended. UK churches need to learn from these churches which have been so successful.

Secondly, although based on very small numbers, the churches in Europe seem to be doing better than might have been expected. The robustness of the numbers is, however, very dubious and it might be better to say that Europe is akin to Latin America, holding its own, rather than doing something spectacular. Even so, this is good news, compared with constant talk of continental decline.

However, even given that, the number of new Christians per day in Europe is pro rata almost the lowest across the world. Europe has 561 million Christians, and the best we can do is to expand by 2,300 a day, two-thirds of whom are born into a Christian family or country! One-and-a-half adult conversions a day per million Christians does not sound too impressive!

Thirdly, the decline in Christianity in North America, which is almost certainly mainly among younger people, is very marked in the table. This is likely to have a number of consequences, as much funding of Christian work world-wide still emanates from North America. The decline may also explain the lack of new initiatives seen in the United States over the last decade. There was Evangelism Explosion in the 1970s, the Willow Creek Community Church in the 1980s and since, and Rick Warren's purpose-driven Saddleback Church in the early 1990s. There does not appear to have been another similar new success story in the last few years, although we cannot discount the incredible over-half-a-century-long ministry of Billy Graham, which began in 1948.

72% community; 8% attendance

The 2001 Population Census in the UK asked a question on religion for the first time for 150 years (except in Northern Ireland, where such a question has been mandatory since the country was established in 1922). Nearly three-quarters of the population, 72%, said they were Christian, higher than many people expected. That percentage was highest in Northern Ireland (86%) and lowest in Scotland (65%). As it was the first time for such a long time that the percentage was counted, we do not know whether it is increasing or decreasing.

However, we do know that the percentage of the population going to church on Sunday in England, Scotland and Wales is decreasing. The percentage attending in Northern Ireland is not known, but is likely to be high. As the Northern Ireland population is small, a high percentage of church attendance there does not actually change the overall UK percentage when taken to the nearest percentage point.

In 1980 11% of the population of Great Britain attended church on Sunday, a percentage which dropped to 10% in 1990 and to 8% in 2000. If present trends continue it is likely to be half that percentage by 2020.

There is obviously a huge gap between profession and attendance. Many people attend church on an occasional basis, and several million go only once a year at Christmas. There are also an increasing number who attend church during the week rather than on Sundays. Allowing for all these, the proportion of the population who may go to church at least once a year could well be 20%,[6] a third of whom go only at Christmas. Even so, there is still a wide gap.

If half the population says they are Christian but never attend a worship service (funerals, weddings and christenings not being counted), what does being a Christian mean in this context? Christianity as a religion naturally has a set of 'theological' beliefs. When measured across the population, they yield the percentages shown in Table 2.2:

Table 2.2
Belief in UK society 1970s–1990s

Belief in . . .	1970s %	1980s %	1990s %
God	74	72	67
Heaven	52	55	52
Life after death	37	43	44
Jesus as the Son of God	55	49	43
Reincarnation	24	26	25
Hell	21	26	25

These figures are broadly consistent with what might be expected of a group of people who say they are Christian. The beliefs of churchgoers are not dramatically different![7] A series of surveys across 39 Anglican congregations[8] in north-west Kent at the beginning of the 21st century with a total attendance of nearly 2,700 people showed that collectively 71% believed that Jesus died for the sins of the world, 68% that He rose from the dead, 67% in God the Father who created the world, 60% in the Trinity, 56% in the empowerment of the Holy Spirit, and 52% that Jesus was the only way to heaven. This suggests that Christian belief does not depend hugely on whether a person goes to church!

Christianity is also a 'moral' religion. That is, Christians are expected to follow the Ten Commandments. They are not expected to cheat, steal, lie, commit adultery, murder, etc. If a person doesn't do these things and is thus living a 'good' life, would he/she describe him/herself as a Christian as a consequence? Could this explain the high percentage of 'Christians' who don't go to church?

What does this mean for churches in the UK? Many people call themselves Christian but do not attend church, even occasionally. This has strategic implications for the preaching of the Gospel. Do we have to think of new ways of presenting the message of Jesus Christ to people who say they are already Christian?

Belief in some of the fundamentals of Christianity is common, and is not much stronger among churchgoers. Should that platform be taken as the starting point or should one reckon on rebuilding the foundation? In other words, how much should be assumed in understanding of Christian belief by those who do not regularly attend church? How should we welcome newcomers?

Perhaps the most important element in this section is the fact that regular church attendance has been declining and is likely to continue to do so. This has major implications for the future pattern of church and the sustainability of present expressions of church. It also suggests that strategic thinking is necessary if the church in the UK is to have a significant future rather than decline into a minority interest with little or no impact on the nation.

Growing churches

Overall church attendance is declining, but this is not universal, and many churches are growing. The evidence from one large survey in England is that the proportion of growing churches is increasing:[9] over the period 1989 to 1998 22% of churches grew,[10] but between 1991 and 2001 30% of churches grew. There is a large overlap in the periods covered by these two surveys, and the fact that the second percentage is higher than the first suggests that most of this additional growth came in the late 1990s or early in the 2000s.

Why do churches grow? Another large survey, also undertaken by Christian Research, looked at the reasons for growth. Two major reasons emerged, but there were a number of subsidiary factors. They are important for strategic reassessment of where a church is heading and the kind of ministry being exercised. They help to define a church's 'culture', or the expectations surrounding a church's work. They are shown in Figure 2.3.[11] Two were particularly important – the warmth of the welcome and the church's ministry, which would include its involvement with the local community. A warm welcome suggests pleasant church people, but 'people don't want a friendly church, they want a friend'.[12]

The latter kind of involvement enables the church to create a 'fringe', a group of people who learn not only where the church is and what it looks like (important for some!), but who also meet church people in some kind of not directly religious way. They watch them, not necessarily consciously, and come to appreciate their values. Such friends of church people frequently respond positively to an invitation to attend a special service or come on an Alpha course, for example.

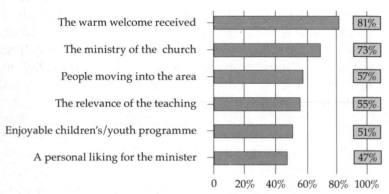

Figure 2.3
Subsidiary reasons for church growth

A congregation of a 100 people will have 5 *visitors* on a typical Sunday.[13] Some might be friends or relatives of existing church people, but others will not be! Visitors to growing churches were more likely to *receive something* than those going to declining churches (68% to 58%). What they received did not seem to matter! It is important, however, that what they take away has contact information on it. Five churches in eight, 62%, have a *welcome team*, one-third of which had had specific training for their work.[14]

Major reasons: leadership and vision

The reasons in Figure 2.3 are labelled 'subsidiary' because the research indicated two overwhelming reasons for growth: the church's vision and the type of leader. 'Shapers' (using Belbin terminology, which is explained in more detail in Chapter 6) are twice as likely to lead a growing church as a declining church.[15] In other words, the driving vision of a minister determined to make it happen proved to be the overriding imperative for growth. How a vision may be developed is explored in later chapters.

Growing churches are also more likely to have the presence of some ethnic minority groups in their congregation than declining churches (62% to 46%). They are also more likely to be charismatic or evangelical (52% to 36%), and to have held an Alpha course (73% to 64%).[16]

What these surveys have shown is that:

- Growing churches are by no means uncommon, even though a majority are in fact still declining.

- Growth often comes through having a culture and activities that are relevant both to those who already attend and to the local community.

- The key reasons for growth relate to the minister rather than to programmes. His/her personality and gifts are crucial, especially in a larger church, where people tend to come not so much because of who the minister is, but more for what he/she does – help people understand, in relevant terms, what Christianity means.

Another key factor is that of worship. People generally prefer a variety of types of worship and styles of music. One survey showed that churches using only an organ were more likely to be declining than growing (76% to 58%).[17] However, variety is not the main consideration: 'People are not looking so much for worship that is relevant as they are for worship that is real.'[18]

Number of leaders

There is another factor, however, of importance in growing churches. They are much more likely to have a small, effective leadership team. The analysis of the Scottish Church Census[19] proved conclusively that growing churches have smaller leadership teams (in that study, an average of 13 people). Stable churches had an average of 19 leaders and declining churches 22 (unless they were declining so fast that they couldn't get enough leaders!).

Church of Scotland churches frequently have many Elders (on average 27)[20] as do Anglicans with their Parochial Church Councils (PCCs). How can such a large number be reduced, when Elders are appointed for life, and the PCC size is largely immutable? One Church of Scotland church in Edinburgh breaks the Eldership down into groups, or committees. Thus there is a Pastoral Committee, a Finance Committee, a Social Committee, and so on. Especially, however, there is an Executive Committee, which consists of about 10 people, and it is this group that effectively runs the church. PCCs could be broken down likewise, with say the Standing Committee (augmented if necessary) equating to the Executive Committee. The Committees meet more frequently than the overall body, and the agenda for the latter is largely receiving reports of the various Committees, but crucially initiating appropriate action.

Generational change

The generation gap is real, important and growing! The proportions by age group of those attending church on Sunday in Great Britain between 1985 and 2005 is shown in Figure 2.4:

Figure 2.4
Proportions attending church in Great Britain by age group
1985–2005

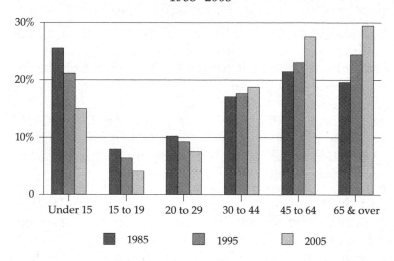

It is obvious that the churches in Britain are losing young people rapidly. That is not a new finding but it is something for which strategic action needs to be taken. Detailed research among those aged 10 to 14 showed that two-thirds of young people in church when aged 12 would leave within 2 years.[21] The figures indicate that across England, Wales and Scotland at the beginning of the 21st century churches were losing 750 children under 15 *per week*! That is equivalent to almost 40,000 a year, which over a decade is 400,000 children. Since in 2005 there will be on current trends only 625,000 children in church, it is very clear that this is a major crisis that will not go away. In terms of thinking about the future this is of high significance. The research[22] suggested that churches urgently begin to appoint children's workers to work with those under 12, just as a decade earlier they had begun to appoint youth workers to work generally with teenagers.

Figure 2.4 also shows that the proportion of those aged 30 or above steadily increases across the years 1985 to 2005. In 1985, those 30 and over were 58% of congregations; by 2005, if present trends continue, they will be 74%.

Radical changes need to be made if the implications of these figures are not to present the church image as a club for old people. Chapter 7 tells how this challenge was put to a Baptist church in Kent, which came up with answers such as holding a café-style service for young people on Saturday evening, or an after-school club for children of families where both parents work. This kind of problem requires careful 'Centre of Gravity' thinking and consideration.

Generational variations

The key variations here lie across the generations, a difference that has been explored in many books.[23] A summary of how these different generations tick, as it were, is given in Table 2.5, with the age range that is normally given to each group, but with the approximate description by age in brackets underneath, as these are easier to consider.

The topology used in Table 2.5 originally came from the United States and centred around their Baby Boom people, a well-above-average number who were born in the late 1940s. Britain experienced a similar boom in births in the late 1950s and early 1960s, and thus conveniently have a group born in the same period as America. These Boomers, as they were called (Baby being dropped fairly quickly), were then seen as a generation, and their children (who broke, or bust, the boom) were called Busters, while Boomer parents were called different names, of which perhaps Builders is the most preferable.

Table 2.5
Generational differences

Generation Name	Builders	Boomers	Generation X	Mosaics
Age in 2004	59 to 77 (60s & over)	40 to 58 (40s & 50s)	21 to 39 (20s & 30s)	2 to 20 (Under 21)
Charac-teristic				
Respect . . .	Status	Competence	Openness	Involvement
Support	Can manage without it	Like it	Need it	Constant contact by mobile
Work	Happy to do any job	More specialist	Look at team first	Own own business
Church	Attend out of habit	Like to use their gifts	Attend when feel like it	What's Christianity?
Think . . .	Linearly and logically		Creatively	Fragmentally

The Busters were also called the Millennium Generation, as the generation which would reach adulthood at the start of the new millennium, or Beepers, as they grew up with the new IT technology. A much more contemporary term quickly caught on in the early 1990s from a book by Douglas Coupland[24] – the X Generation or Generation X. Many other books and articles have followed about this generation.

Their children somewhat naturally are called Generation Y, but they have also been called other names, of which Mosaics is the most common, since their worldview is made up of scattered pieces, each part of the total picture, like a Roman mosaic. *Their* children, Generation Z, may also be called the 'Kaleidoscopes', since they are likely to make more than one picture (or worldview) with the pieces they put together.

The value of this kind of topology is that it can conveniently be used to describe some of the different characteristics for each generation. Table 2.5 summarises some of the key characteristics which may be of value to church leaders thinking through how different generations can be encouraged to attend church or how they may want to be involved.

Thus, for example, Table 2.5 shows that while Builders, many of whom are now retired, were happy to do any job (they needed the money!), Boomers preferred jobs which fitted their gifting or speciality (they could usually do a good job, therefore). Generation Xers, on the other hand, want firstly to know with whom they will be working rather than details about the job itself – company counts! Mosaics don't mind working in teams, but prefer independence, or at least the ability to do things the way they want, and running their own organisation fits this very neatly.

This can be seen in a church context. Many Builders, those in their 60s or over, are more than happy to do anything useful in a church to help things along. Those in their 40s and 50s want to do jobs that fit their gifting, which creates problems if there aren't enough teachers for the Sunday school! Those in their 20s and 30s think of their group and who else is in the team, because their interest lies in the interactions between these people. Since many churches struggle to have sufficient numbers in this age group to form a realistic team, frustration can abound. And young people want to do things that are challenging and unconventional – presumably why midnight hikes and bungee jumping are so popular!

Evangelical growth

The second English Church Census took place on Sunday 15th October 1989 with a form being sent to all 38,000 churches in England. A total of 70% of these were returned – an unprecedented response. This included a 75% response from Anglican churches, an important group since their changes are different from others. The English Church Attendance Survey in September 1998 was not answered as well, attracting only a half of the previous response.

One of the questions in 1989 asked the minister to describe the churchmanship of the congregation. This question was answered by 89%, thus giving the churchmanship of nearly 11,000 Church of England churches and of 13,000 churches of other denominations.

Table 2.6 is a complicated table but essentially it is showing the number of churches and number of church-goers (the Base figures) and the proportions of both which were evangelical in both 1989 and 1998. It is divided into four quarters, one each for Anglicans, Roman Catholics, all other denominations, and the overall total.

It may be read in the following way, starting with the Anglican quarter. In 1989 18% of Anglican churches were evangelical, based on the 16,373 churches the Anglicans then had. During the next nine years to 1998, some churches ceased to be evangelical, but a greater number changed in the opposite direction. Therefore, by 1998 22% of Anglican churches[25] counted themselves as evangelical, based on 16,281 churches.

The next two lines show the percentage of Anglican churchgoers who were evangelical in 1989 and 1998, and again there was an increase – from 26% to 35%. The numbers on which they are based are also given.

Table 2.6
English evangelical churches and churchgoers, 1989 and 1998

		Anglicans		Roman Catholics	
		1989	1998	1989	1998
	Churches	*18%*	*22%*	*1%*	*3%*
	Base	16,373	16,281	3,824	3,771
	Churchgoers	*26%*	*35%*	$\frac{1}{3}$*%*	*4%*
	Base	1,266,300	980,600	1,715,900	1,230,100
Average } congregation }	Evangelicals	113	94	148	435
	Non-evangelicals	70	51	452	322
		All others		TOTAL	
	Churches	*58%*	*61%*	*35%*	*38%*
	Base	18,410	17,665	38,607	37,717
	Churchgoers	*62%*	*66%*	*30%*	*37%*
	Base	1,760,600	1,504,000	4,742,800	3,714,700
Average } congregation }	Evangelicals	102	93	105	96
	Non-evangelicals	86	74	133	100

If one knows the number of churchgoers and the number of churches, an easy division gives the size of the average congregation. These are given in the bottom section of each quarter, where for comparison the average size of non-evangelical congregations is also given.

The same pattern works in the other quarters. The Catholic figures are based on small numbers, but because they have much larger churches than Protestants, unfortunately they make the overall total figures less meaningful. They will, however, be of interest to charismatic Catholics (as evangelical Catholics invariably call themselves). The 'All others' include Baptists, Methodists, United Reformed, Pentecostal, New, Independent churches, etc.

From all of this, it may be seen that:

- The proportion of evangelical *churches* has increased, whether you look at Anglicans, Catholics or all the others, despite a declining number of churches. The Anglicans have increased most.

- The proportion of evangelical *churchgoers* has also increased, again across the board, and has increased faster than the proportion of churches. So the evangelical churches are growing more than non-evangelical ones. Again, the increase among the Anglicans is greatest.

- The average evangelical congregation is larger than non-evangelical congregations (except for the Catholics in 1989). Again, the change in Anglican congregations is the most dramatic, with 1998 evangelical congregations being almost double the size of non-evangelical churches (94 to 51). That the same proportion did not hold in 1989 (113 to 70) shows that the Anglican evangelicals have considerably increased their strength during the 1990s – an encouraging legacy for the Anglican Archbishop of that period, George Carey?

If present trends continue, and they may well not do so (trends are very rarely uniform), then the proportion of Sunday churchgoers in the Church of England in, say, 2010 who are evangelical could increase from 35% to 50%.

The Anglican 35% in 1998 compares unfavourably, however, with the two-thirds, 66%, in all the other denominations who are already evangelical, a percentage that is also growing, and, if present trends continue, could reach 72% by 2010.

The total percentages do not reflect these high percentages and strengths because the number of Roman Catholics is large and the proportion who are evangelical very small, although again growing. Taking the Anglicans and other denominations together, then for these the evangelical percentage has grown from 47% in 1989 to 54% in 1998, and could reach 64% by 2010. One element of the big picture that church leaders have to take into consideration is this current evangelical growth.

The implications for Anglicans are wider still. A sample of almost a third of their clergy showed that 47% had trained at an evangelical theological college, and that because evangelical churches had larger congregations the church's average income was double that of non-evangelical Anglican churches (£84,000 to £40,000).[26]

Size of churches

The size of a church is important. We have already seen in Figure 1.1 how this impacts leadership. In England there are 38,000 churches. Catholic churches are almost always larger than Protestant ones,[27] so when looking at size a clearer picture is given if the 4,000 Catholic churches are excluded. 50% of the Protestant churchgoers attended just 15% of their 34,000 churches in 1998,[28] with an average congregation of 270. The other 50% of people attend 85% of churches, with an average congregation of 70!

Environment

This is partly because many English churches, 42%, are in rural areas where the average congregation is 30. A third, 35%, of Church of England churches are in remoter rural areas that had an average congregation of only 10 people in 1998.[29]

In Scotland there are 4,100 churches. 50% of the Protestant churchgoers attend 34% of the churches with an average attendance of 240; the remaining 50% attend 66% of churches with an average attendance of 120, almost twice that of the English smaller churches. The rural churches in Scotland are much better attended than English rural churches, with an average of 80 attenders.

Larger churches

The proportion of larger churches grew in the 1990s in England, as Table 2.7 indicates:

Table 2.7
Proportions of Protestant churches and churchgoers
by size of church, 1989 and 1998

Sunday attendance	Churches		Churchgoers	
	1989 %	1998 %	1989 %	1998 %
50 or under	38	47	12	13
51 to 100	25	26	20	19
101 to 200	29	18	42	33
201 to 400	7	7	19	25
over 400	1.3	1.5	7	10

This table (which again excludes the Catholics) shows that the proportion of churches with less than 50 people on a Sunday grew between 1989 and 1998, but the proportion that declined had between 100 and 200, which agrees with the analysis of Bob Jackson[30] of Anglican churches.

The proportion of those *attending* churches with under 100, 32% in total, did not change, however, between 1989 and 1998. What did change was the proportion attending churches with congregations in excess of 200. The largest churches of all, with regular congregations in excess of 400, are an important sub-section of these. 10% of all churchgoers attend just 1.5% of Free and Anglican churches, churches with an average Sunday congregation of 480 people.

About a quarter of the overall total of these largest churches are Church of England, where they constituted about 1% of the total number of churches but 8% of attenders in 1998. Virtually all of them are mainstream evangelical, and, at the time of writing, all are led by men, although there are women in their leadership teams. In America these largest churches are called 'megachurches'. Eddie Gibbs writes, 'Megachurches carry an enormous responsibility for the future of Christianity ... because of the rapidly increasing percentage of churchgoers being attracted to a small number of megachurches.'[31]

Characteristics of larger churches

What makes larger churches large? They are usually very busy churches with lots of activities. As a consequence, they reach into the local community and are able to engage in effective evangelism by building on these contacts. Perhaps a third of their growth comes from conversions. In addition:

- Their leaders think strategically.
- They provide practical discipleship opportunities, so that people can grow in their faith.
- They are able to delegate pastoral care, and have a structure for that, sometimes through house groups.
- The preaching helps people 'understand what the Bible means', as a lady in one focus group put it.
- They are friendly churches, providing a warm welcome, and their people can quickly make friends.
- All life-stages are present, so that single mums can find other single mums; empty nesters (when children have

left the home) can share with others like them; there is a range of activities for those with children; there will be a group unmarried people can attend.

- If necessary, though, there will be the opportunity to be anonymous for those who just want to watch and consider.

Leadership in these churches is crucial. The personality of the minister effectively directs the church's culture, and his gifting will often be a main attraction if he is a good teacher. His motivations, of achieving and affiliating, drive the church. He also needs to be a good team leader and have a clear vision! Although he is not perfect, the minister will have a distinct set of gifts, which the rest of this book describes.

Growing churches

Large churches are not the same as growing churches (already considered), although as most large churches *are* growing there will be many characteristics in common. Churches of whatever size can grow; size is not the make-or-break factor, leadership and vision are. It is these that characterise the leaders of growing churches.

Changing patterns of church

Church life is changing! In the late 1990s I asked the leader of a large church how he thought churches would change over the next decade. He answered without hesitation, 'Oh, we will be having our regular worship on Thursday evenings. Sunday mornings will only attract those who like to sing!' While this is doubtless an exaggeration, some of that movement is already happening.

Declining frequency

The frequency with which people, even committed Christians, attend church is declining. Of those who attend church at least monthly, the proportion coming twice on a Sunday is definitely reducing, from 16% in 1985 to 14% in 1989 to 12% in 1998.[32] 10% of the population attended church in England in 1989, the large majority of whom went every Sunday. By 1998 the percentage had reduced to 7.5% (now more accurately 7.6%, as the Office for National Statistics has found the population was not as big as originally claimed! We will continue to use the 7.5% since this is the percentage most people remember). A third of that 2.5% reduction between 1989 and 1998 was simply due to people attending less frequently.

The 7.5% broke down into two groups: those who really did come every week, 4.4%, and those who came less frequently but who happened to be present that Sunday in September 1998 when everyone was counted, 3.1%. Over the course of a month there will be more 'casual' attenders who actually come, amounting to 5.8% of the population.

This percentage of 5.8% of the population when added to the regular 4.4% makes a total of 10.2%, which is the percentage of the population who attend church at least once a month.

So, apart from those going every week, almost twice as many people attend church once a month as come on a typical Sunday. The regularity of attendance is nothing like as uniform as it was, and the change has largely taken place over the 1990s. One vicar said, 'The people who used to come twice on Sunday now come twice a month.'

Importance of midweek

As well as a declining frequency, there is also the pheno-menon of midweek attendance. Numerous churches have long held midweek services, but most of the attenders in the past also came on Sundays. The change that has occurred, again largely in the 1990s, is that many of the midweek attenders now no longer attend on Sunday as well. The importance of this activity is greater in Scotland than in England: in Scotland for every 3 people in church on Sunday there will be one coming midweek [and not on Sunday]; in England for every 10 people on Sunday there is one coming midweek.

These two studies were measured four years apart, Scotland in 2002 and England in 1998. As the change to midweek is actively happening it may well be that by 2002 a higher proportion than 10% of English churchgoers would have been attending only during the week.

What brings people along midweek? There are three types of activities. Worship services are particularly common in the more liturgical churches and are held by 56% of Scottish churches and 42% of English ones.[33] Average attendance was 27 in Scotland and 21 in England, accounting for respectively 0.6% and 0.7% of the population (this way round as there are more churches to the population in England than in Scotland). In Scotland the most popular time and day was 7.00 p.m. on Wednesdays; the question wasn't asked in England.

Then there are the midweek activities that many churches have. These may be luncheon clubs, mums and toddlers' groups, Bible studies, after-school clubs. The variety is enormous; many churches are actively involved in the life of their local community. The average attendance, cumulating across all types of activity, was 73 in a typical week in Scotland and 70 in England.[34] It is no real surprise that women tend to come more than men to midweek activities. More churches had such activities in England than in Scotland, 45% to 33%.

The third type of midweek activities are those that are explicitly for young people (in this context those under 25). They could have been included in the second category but are so important that it is best to consider them separately. In Scotland 47% of churches ran youth activities; the percentage is not known for England. The Scottish youth activities were mostly youth *clubs*, which young people preferred to attend rather than church! Only 14% of those coming midweek to these went to church as well.[35]

A separate study[36] asked the young people why they preferred going midweek.

- The answer was that there was *food* midweek!
- It was *fun* midweek! One English lad said, 'No-one ever laughs in church. Perhaps they should have a Happy Week!'[37]
- They were also *free* from their parents midweek! They went alone or with friends, whereas for most they were 'taken' by their parents on Sunday.
- They were also *free* to choose whether or not they went midweek. They nearly always chose to go, but it was their choice, not their parents'.

Changing church culture

There are many other examples of how church life is changing.[38] We have not even mentioned such phenomena as Cell Church, Emerging Church, Liquid Church or Alternative Worship, mainly because little if any research has been done into their long-term impact. Addressing Synod in July 2003, the Archbishop of Canterbury, Most Reverend Rowan Williams, said:

At present there is actually an extraordinary amount going on in terms of the creation of new styles of church life. We can call it church planting, 'new ways of being church' or various other things; but the point is that more and more patterns of worship and shared life are appearing on the edge of our mainstream life that cry out for our support, understanding and nurture if they are not to get isolated and unaccountable.[39]

Absolutely! And it is one of the most exciting and potentially vital changes in British church life. It is literally life and culture changing!

So what?

One of the characteristics of strategic leadership is the ability to 'look at trends and take appropriate leverage action'. Seven trends have been described in this chapter. Which of these are relevant in your situation? If you wish to add one not mentioned (or several others) by all means do. *Tick* those relevant in the table below. Then, looking at just those you have ticked, *circle* the one that has the highest importance impacting your situation.

Table 2.8
Seven trends

World-wide church growth	☐
Increasing Christian nominality in UK	☐
Increasing numbers of growing churches	☐
Ever widening generation gap	☐
Growing numbers of evangelicals	☐
Increasing importance of larger churches	☐
Changing patterns of church life	☐
Other:	☐

What action(s) do you need to take in order to work through the implications of the item you have circled?

Notes

[1] Auguste Rodin's *The Thinker* was originally completed in 1880, was cast in bronze in 1960 and now stands outside Stanford University, United States.

[2] *Management Today*, June 2003, pp. 10, 11.

[3] Mrs Jill Garrett was the speaker at the CEO Forum arranged jointly by the Evangelical Alliance and Christian Research on 26th September 2000.

[4] Dr Peter Brierley, *The Impact of Society upon the Church* (London: Christian Research, 2001).

[5] Dr David Barrett, 'Status of Global Mission 2003', *International Bulletin of Missionary Research*, January 2003, p. 25.

[6] 'Christmas 2002', *Quadrant*, Bulletin of Christian Research, November 2002, p. 3.

[7] This begs the question of whether the general population's belief in God can be equated with the belief in God revealed in the Scriptures and more likely to be held by churchgoers.

[8] Using the Congregational Attitudes and Beliefs Survey in the Deaneries of Erith, Orpington and Sidcup in the Diocese of Rochester, undertaken by Christian Research between 1999 and 2001.

[9] *The Mind of Anglicans* study, undertaken by Christian Research for Cost of Conscience in 2002.

[10] *Church Growth in the 1990s*, survey undertaken by Christian Research for Springboard, Abingdon, Oxon., 2000.

[11] Taken from Peter Brierley (ed.), *Religious Trends* No. 4, 2003/2004 (London: Christian Research, 2003), Table 5.2.1.

[12] George Barna, *Grow Your Church from the Outside* (Ventura, California: Regal, 2002).

[13] Peter Brierley, *The Tide is Running Out: What the English Church Attendance Survey Reveals* (London: Christian Research, 2000), p. 75.

[14] Taken from Peter Brierley, *Leadership, Vision and Church Growth* (London: Christian Research, 2003), giving extracts of some results from a survey undertaken on behalf of the Salvation Army Central North Division in 2002, p. 11.

[15] Ibid., p. 6.

[16] Brierley (ed.), *Religious Trends* No. 4, Table 5.3.2.

[17] *Leadership, Vision and Church Growth*, p. 20.

[18] Eddie Gibbs and Ian Coffey, *ChurchNext* (IVP, Nottingham, 2001), p. 155.

[19] Peter Brierley, *Turning the Tide: The Challenge Ahead – The Results of the 2002 Scottish Church Census* (Edinburgh: Church of Scotland, and London: Christian Research, 2003), p. 91.

[20] Ibid., p. 122.

[21] Peter Brierley, *Reaching and Keeping Tweenagers* (London: Christian Research, 2003).

[22] Ibid., p. 192.

[23] For example, Kath Donovan, *From Separation to Synergy: Receiving the Richness of Generation X*, Zadok Paper S106, Zadok Institute, Winter 2000; George Barna, *Generation NeXt* (Ventura, California: Regal, 1995); Peter Brierley, *Generation X: Attitudes and Lifestyles* Survey Report, Christian Research, March 2001; Nick Pollard, *Why do they do that? Understanding Teenagers* (Oxford: Lion, 1998); Rick and Kathy Hicks, *Boomers, Xers, and Other Strangers* (Nottingham: Tyndale, 1999); Mark Henderson, 'Generation Y: Young, Gifted and Self-centred', *The Times*, 14th November 1998; and Brierley, *Reaching and Keeping Tweenagers*, ch. 1.

[24] Douglas Coupland, *Generation X: Tales from an Accelerated Culture* (New York: St Martin's Press, 1991).

[25] Brierley, *The Tide is Running Out*, Table 41, p. 146.

[26] Peter Brierley, 'The Strategic Importance of Evangelical Anglicans', *Church of England Newspaper*, 3rd July 2003, p. 18.

[27] Anglican churches are counted here as Protestant churches, a description that not all accept.

[28] Brierley, *The Tide is Running Out*, p. 49.

[29] Peter Brierley (ed.), *Religious Trends* No. 3, 2002/2003 (London: Christian Research, 2001), Tables 2.24.2, 3.

[30] Revd Bob Jackson, *Hope for the Church: Contemporary Strategies for Growth* (London: Church House Publishing, 2002).

[31] Gibbs and Coffey, *ChurchNext*, p. 74.

[32] Brierley, *The Tide is Running Out*, p. 79.

[33] Brierley, *Turning the Tide*, p. 95.

[34] Made up of 41 adults and 32 children under 15 in Scotland, and 37 adults and 33 children in England.

[35] Brierley, *Turning the Tide*, p. 100.

[36] *Ministry Among Young People*, Study for the Church of Scotland Parish Education Department by Christian Research, London, Autumn 2000.

[37] Brierley, *Reaching and Keeping Tweenagers*, pp. 110, 129.

[38] Some were given in a little booklet, *12 Ideas to Help Turn the Tide*, produced by Christian Research, London, 2001.

[39] Article in Synod Observer Section, 'Archbishop Sets Out his Vision', *Church of England Newspaper*, 17th July 2003.

Chapter 3

The Invisible and Vision
in Leadership

In a key book on leadership, Oswald Sanders, then the General Director of the mission agency OMF International, wrote:

> Eyes that look are common. Eyes that see are rare. The Pharisees looked at Peter and saw only a poor unlettered fisherman, totally insignificant, not worthy of a second look. Jesus saw Peter and discovered the prophet and preacher, saint and leader of the unique band of men who turned the world upside down.[1]

What invisible things did Jesus see in Peter that the Pharisees didn't? Very few people naturally look beyond the obvious. Jesus did so again and again, but there are other examples in the Bible. Take Abraham: he looked at the length and breadth of the land in Genesis 13 and saw (because God had revealed it to him) a nation and an inheritance. He looked at innumerable stars in Genesis 15 and saw countless descendants; he looked at the Lord in Genesis 18 and saw justice; he looked at the ram in Genesis 22 and saw God's provision for the sacrifice rather than his son, Isaac; he looked at rural hills or desert most of his life but Hebrews 11:10 tells us that he saw 'the city which has foundations'. It would be fascinating to know how

Abraham learned to translate the visible into the invisible, but it was his ability to do so which made him the founder of a nation.

A leader has to see the invisible in order to discover vision, otherwise it is not vision but good forward planning. The Bible tells us and our senses confirm that God is 'invisible' (1 Tim. 1:17), though sometimes men and women are permitted unique manifestations of Him. The invisible is an essential element to leadership and vision, and one way to explore it is by looking at the experience of three Old Testament leaders.

Moses

Moses was an amazing example of the verse in Proverbs 'Train up a child in the way he should go, and when he is old, he will not depart from it' (Prov. 22:6). One imagines that the writer of the proverb anticipated that the parents would be the ones to train the child, but after Moses was taken to Pharaoh's palace his parents effectively became invisible. Maybe he saw them occasionally (some Jewish traditions suggest quite frequently), but by the time they died he had probably fled out of Egypt to get away from Pharaoh. This family was probably largely invisible for the formative years of his life, yet shaped his destiny.

Somewhere in his education, equivalent to going to a top school and university today, Moses learned invisible values alongside Egyptian ones. He was taught the economics of affluence, but he also learned the economics of equality. He was taught the politics of oppression, but he also learned the politics of justice. He was taught a religion of immanence and accessibility, but he also learned a religion of God's freedom.[2]

He ran away from Pharaoh's supposed wrath when he was about 40 years of age. The enmity of his former guardian was invisible too, though real – God had to reassure Moses that 'all the men who were seeking your life are dead' (Ex. 4:19). Only when the pressure from the invisible threat was lifted would he consider returning. It was 'not Pharaoh only that had vanished out of his sight ... Moses himself had disappeared. He had broken down when he trusted himself. He now endures because he saw nought but God.'[3]

His call to service

Some 40 years after running away, Moses spoke with the invisible God, represented by flames, which captured his attention because they burnt in a bush without consuming it.[4] 'Fire is an emblem of deity',[5] but Moses heard God's voice and had a real conversation with Him, even though he hid his face, being afraid even to look at the fiery symbol of God's living presence (Ex. 3:6). He was 'not frightened or repelled by the sight but drawn towards it, though not for religious reasons. Moses is simply curious ... Curiosity leads to call.'[6]

It took another amazing further 40 years of incredible fortitude and persistence for him to lead the band of escaped slaves to the edge of the Promised Land. That key work of his life is summarised in the New Testament as '[Moses] endured as seeing Him who is invisible' (Heb. 11:27). This 'does not mean he saw God with the naked eye. Faith's eye saw what the physical eye is incapable of seeing.'[7]

The invisible for Moses

Living with the invisible was part of Moses' life experience. Some have argued that 'seeing "Him who is invisible" is ordinary, normal Christianity'.[8] However, another Old Testament character shows us that seeing the invisible is not always the norm. Elisha actually had to pray that his servant would also be able to see the surrounding chariots and horses of fire that he could see (2 Kgs. 6:17).

Although Moses ran away at 40 because he was afraid, and he was so terrified of facing Pharaoh at age 80 that God had to allow Aaron to be his spokesman, ultimately Moses' experience of the invisible made him *unafraid*, as clearly his parents had been when they hid him for three months (Heb. 11:23). It also gave him *confidence* in his leadership, although he was sometimes over-venturesome, as when he struck the rock to get water (Num. 20:11). He was conscious too of a substantial *reality*, the 'reality of God and of the reward He bestows in response to active faith'.[9]

Moses' sister, Miriam, was called a prophet(ess) (Ex. 15:20) as was his brother, Aaron (Ex. 7:1), but it was only towards the end of his life that Moses is given this appellation. Then he became the quintessential prophet such that God could point to him as a forerunner of Jesus and say that He would 'raise up a prophet like you from among their brethren' (Deut. 18:18). A prophet (importantly referred to as a *seer* in 1 Sam. 9:9) sees the invisible and proclaims it. Was it Moses' experience of seeing the invisible for all those years that made him a prophet?

Walter Brueggemann argues that 'the task of prophetic ministry is to nurture, nourish and evoke a consciousness and perception alternative to the consciousness and perception of the dominant culture around us'.[10] This is precisely what Moses was called to do in his leadership of the Israelites. His vision was to transform a large group of slaves into a nation whose values reflected those of the God who was delivering them from Egypt and providing them with a new land to live in. Moses constantly had to challenge them to think differently and not fall back into the habits they had had in Egypt. Leadership vision focuses on the future state, not on past experience. Moses' sense of the invisible was critical to this process, and his strategy devolved from it.

Taking this more widely, Brueggemann continues: 'Prophetic ministry has not to do primarily with addressing specific public crises, but with addressing, in season and out of season, the dominant crisis that is enduring and resilient.'[11] What, then, is that crisis and the prophetic ministry that must address it? Brueggemann would say it was 'to contradict a situation of hopelessness', 'to bring to public expression [the] hopes and yearnings that have been denied so long' and 'to penetrate the despair so that new futures can be believed'.[12] It seems to me that what he describes as 'prophetic ministry' is very akin in scope to 'strategic thinking', which needs to have similar aims – understanding of the present, communication of hope and verbally depicting believable outcomes.

The example of Isaiah

Moses' response is paralleled by the experience of the prophet Isaiah some 600 years later. Isaiah was also given a task so difficult that, like Moses, he could easily have become depressed. His call was to 'Go, and say to this people: "Hear and hear, but do not understand; see and see, but do not perceive"' (Is. 6:9). One commentator has translated this as:

> Hear continually, yet gain no insight, and
> See unceasingly, but do not achieve understanding.[13]

The implication is that 'the disease of pride and rebellion has gone so deeply that they will simply misperceive the truth of what they hear',[14] something Brueggemann would support, and which echoes the people described in 2 Timothy as those 'who will listen to anybody and can never arrive at a knowledge of the truth' (3:7). This problem is still with us – many simply cannot hear anything outside the box of their own experience. To put it another way, they are neither interested in nor aroused by the communication of hope and so are sceptical of the future they hear described.

Thus the nub of the invisible strategy of Moses (what we will later call the Centre of Gravity) was so to change the Israelite understanding that they could embrace the future God was promising them. It is the tragedy of the story (but not the fault of Moses) that in the end only Joshua and Caleb amongst those aged over 20 were able to understand and respond with faith. Perhaps in Isaiah's day it was a similar minute fraction who understood what he was saying – with the large majority so infuriated that, if tradition is correct, they actually sawed him in half to silence him (cf. Heb. 11:37).

Hezekiah

Isaiah was the key prophet for King Hezekiah, giving him advice, prayer support and the assurance he needed. The intimacy between them described in the Bible suggests they got on well. Hezekiah was a God-fearing, believing king, willing to take risks for the sake of God's people. 'There was none like him among all the kings of Judah' (2 Kgs. 18:5), and he is the only king whose history is told three times in Scripture.

Stand against the Assyrians

It was Hezekiah who saw the siege and fall of neighbouring Samaria between 711 and 709 BC when he was 33 to 35 years old. When Jerusalem's turn came eight years later, he stood against the might of the Assyrian Emperor and swore not to give in. He heard but was not swayed by the defiant words of human power and conquest (which were true) and the cynical comments of how the Israelite's God could do nothing to save them (which were untrue). He gave courageous leadership under enormous pressure, which resulted in a decisive victory. Sennacherib lost his army, probably due to bubonic plague or something similar. He went home and did not venture towards Judah again in the remaining 20 years of his life before he was murdered by two of his sons (when Manasseh was king). Chapters 36 and 37 of Isaiah are compelling reading!

Hezekiah's firm stand was during a siege, which went on for many weeks. The physical and psychological reaction afterwards was similar to that of Elijah after his great confrontation with the prophets of Baal on Mount Carmel (1 Kgs. 17). Elijah ran away and sank into despair. Hezekiah became ill (Is. 38), so ill that he was on the point of death. The Assyrians had had to take priority, a very pressing priority, but actually Hezekiah had other, invisible, and more urgent priorities. He had begun to change the worship culture of the Israelite nation (2 Kgs. 18:4). When he fell ill, he mourned that he hadn't finished the job (his prayer in Isaiah 38 is not repeated elsewhere). God told Isaiah that He would give Hezekiah a further 15 years to do more to fulfil his vision (verse 5), and that he would therefore recover. While his aides applied an antiseptic (verse 21) to aid the healing process, Hezekiah wanted to know whether God supported his crusade. He did! The sun that day went back ten degrees, physical and incontrovertible evidence to Hezekiah that God was behind him.

Hezekiah's family

There is something strange about Hezekiah's family. His father, King Ahaz, who came to the throne when he was just 20 years old, died when he was 36. In those 16 years he introduced child sacrifice, one of 'the abominable practices of the nations whom the Lord drove out ... of Israel' (2 Chron. 28:3). He also suffered defeat by the Syrians, paid the Assyrians to help him, although their efforts 'did not help him' (2 Chron. 28:21), and took down parts of the Temple.

Hezekiah was born when Ahaz was still a child of 11 years of age, and came to the throne when he was 25. So in his impressionable years from nine to 25 he watched his father act as sovereign. It would have been natural for him to follow his father in his policies and actions, but he didn't:

> When Hezekiah assumed sole control of the Kingdom, he knew exactly how he was going to approach the problem ... to look for help in the one place where it was to be found ... More than that, Hezekiah accepted the crisis as a positive challenge.[15]

Somewhere Hezekiah had what today would be called a conversion. He came to know the Lord deeply, sufficiently deeply to embrace an invisible agenda of seeking to return the Israelites to their true religious heritage. He was given that opportunity when he was 25, and was allowed to follow it for 29 years until his death at 54. He was 39 when God granted him an extra 15 years, which in effect doubled the length of his reign. 'Hezekiah's actions came from his "heart" [NRSV], that is, his will.'[16] 'His own devotion to royal obligations'[17] was not derived from his father.

However, neither was it copied by his son. It was during those extra 15 years that Hezekiah's first son, Manasseh, was born, when Hezekiah was 42. Manasseh therefore came to the throne when he was a child of 12 and presumably had not had long enough to grasp fully what his father was about. Did that give a chance to the many royal advisers to tell him what they wanted instead? Manasseh was one of the kings of Judah who lived longest. He died when he was 67 after a very long reign of 55 years, almost double that of his father. Unfortunately, he totally reversed all that his father had attempted to do in the religious sphere, returning to the worship of Baal and shedding much innocent blood (2 Kgs. 21:3,16), although he seems to have had some kind of death-bed conversion (2 Chron. 33:19).

Manasseh must have despaired of ever producing a male offspring. His son, Josiah, was eventually born when he was 59 years of age, and so came to the throne when just eight years old, even younger than his father. He reigned for 31 years, just a little longer than his grandfather, Hezekiah. If Manasseh hadn't learned from Hezekiah, Josiah probably also learned little from Manasseh in the brief eight years before his father died and he became king. But as a boy-king 'he began to seek the God of David his father' (2 Chron. 34:3). When he was 12 he started to take down the high places, and when he was 26 made a public covenant to the Lord and reintroduced the Passover celebrations. Before Josiah 'there was no king like him, who turned to the Lord with all his heart', soul and might (2 Kgs. 23:25). So it was a real tragedy when he needlessly felt he should tackle the Egyptian Pharaoh Neco on his way to battle the Assyrian Emperor in 609 BC, and died doing so, aged 39.

Heathen Ahaz, godly Hezekiah, heathen Manasseh, godly Josiah. A strange sequence of 131 years of royal power, behind which stands the overarching strategy of God, but within which each king in his own way sought to fulfil his own strategy of change. Neither Ahaz nor Hezekiah lived long enough to see their grandsons, and so could not have personally influenced them.

Hezekiah's passion

Hezekiah began his reforms promptly, in the first month of his reign (2 Chron. 29:3). He put in motion the cleaning and repairs of the Temple and publicly stated his desire 'to make a covenant with the Lord' (verse 10). This heart's desire was his invisible agenda. The Temple was where he found God, so he reinaugurated true worship. He then set about a very careful planning of a recommissioning service for the Temple. He followed the precedent set out by David (verse 25), was personally involved in the process when he gave the order for sacrifices to begin (verse 27) and completed the public follow-through by challenging the people to get involved (verse 31).

This strategy was soon augmented with the reintroduction of the Passover, even though for practical reasons it happened a month later than it should (30:13). Hezekiah knew God well enough to know His directions could be adapted occasionally (reality took priority over rules).

Hezekiah illustrates the key factors in strategy and leadership. The invisible is not as obvious in his life as it was in Moses'. But we can clearly see Hezekiah's long-term vision, detailed strategy, personal walk with God and hidden agenda (the Centre of Gravity again) epitomised very closely in the Military Model we shall later describe!

The strategy was worked out in various ways. There was personal obedience (2 Kgs. 18:6), a discontinuing of former political allegiances (verse 7), victory over nearby enemies (verse 8), who then paid tribute, so building national wealth (2 Chron. 32:27). He purified the land (2 Chron. 31:1), restored Levitical order and civil administration (verses 2 and 4) and reorganised the priests (verses 11–19).

When he learned of the siege of neighbouring Samaria and how the Assyrian commander Sennacherib took the city, he knew Jerusalem's turn would come. A vital strategic preparation was to deprive the Assyrians of water and simultaneously ensure Jerusalem's supply, so he diverted the surface streams and built a tunnel to bring water into the city (2 Chron. 32:30). He was no mean general of his armed forces (2 Chron. 32:3), and planned victory over a much larger fighting force. While he gave the Assyrian commander Sennacherib gold, he also went to the Lord in the Temple (Is. 37:1).

> When there is a financial crisis, the first thing we think about is money. When there is a communications crisis, our prime concern is to learn how to talk the language of the modern generation. When there is a church attendance crisis, we make it our chief aim to get the numbers up. If Hezekiah had responded to a military threat in a military way, the Assyrians would have understood that. Army would have been matched against army, with dire consequences for Judah. But instead he looked first up to God.[18]

Hezekiah coped with the crisis by looking 'not to the threat, nor to the threatened, but to God who was over both'.[19] That is the ability to think strategically from a spiritual perspective, something essential for Christian leaders. No wonder one later commentator writes, 'Wilcock's comment is perceptive and applicable'.[20]

In summary then, Hezekiah had:

- A personal, deep, spiritual devotion to God; God spoke with him (Is. 38:15)
- A faith which developed over time (he started in his first month)
- An ability to see above the problems, huge though they were
- An overall prime trust in God, but he also trusted the people (the priests) and his strategy (his rebuilding plans)
- An ability to take decisive action (like discontinuing the tribute to the Assyrians)

Hezekiah was 'a remarkable shepherd-king pastoring his flock through one of the most critical periods of [Judah's] history'.[21] He worked in a strategic partnership with God, which his grandson followed. He had a personal search for God when he became king (2 Chron. 34:3), ten years before the Book of the Law was discovered.

Daniel

While not that far distant in time, the world of Daniel is aeons away from the world of Hezekiah and his grandson, Josiah. Josiah died in 609 BC, and Pharaoh imposed Jehoiakim as King of Judah (2 Chron. 36:4). He reigned for 11 years from when he was 25 to when Nebuchadnezzar took him to Babylon in 598 BC aged 36 (verse 7). 'The book of Daniel begins with a chronological problem that has always troubled commentators',[22] but 'at some point between the defeat of the Egyptians at the battle of Carchemish in May/June 605 and the death of his father Nabopolassar in August, Nebuchadnezzar subdued Jerusalem and took captives, including Daniel and his three friends'.[23]

Seven years later, in 598 BC, Nebuchadnezzar acted like Pharoah and imposed a new King of Judah, Zedekiah, who was 21 years old (2 Chron. 36:11), and who also reigned for 11 years. He didn't do very well either and was forced to watch his sons being killed before Nebuchadnezzar blinded him and took him also to Babylon (2 Kgs. 25:7) in 586 BC in the final denouement of Jerusalem.

Nabopolassar was the founder of the Chaldean dynasty, which lasted from 625 to 539 BC, when Belshazzar was overcome by the Persians. Nabopolassar's son Nebuchadnezzar reigned from 605 to 562 BC, a long, strong reign of 43 years.

Suppose Daniel was 15 when he was taken to Babylon.[24] He would then have been born in 620 BC and would have been 17 when confronted by Nebuchadnezzar's dream, recorded in Daniel 2. He would have been 35 when Nebuchadnezzar built his huge statue in 585 BC, recorded in Daniel 3 (as a heathen celebration of his victory over Judah), and 51 in 569 BC[25] when Nebuchadnezzar had his second dream, recorded in Daniel 4.

Nebuchadnezzar died in 562 BC and the following few years are tangled. His son, Evil-Merodach, reigned for two years but was killed by his elderly brother-in-law, Neriglassar, who ascended the throne but died in 556 BC. In his turn, he was succeeded by his son, who was dethroned after two months by Nabonidus, who reigned until 539 BC. Nabonidus, however, decided to live in Teima in the Arabian desert for ten years, so in 553 BC Belshazzar became co-regent, when about 37 years of age.[26]

Daniel's working life lasted from when he was about 18 to when he was 82, the first year of Cyrus the Persian (Dan. 1:21). Of those 63 years, the majority (two-thirds or 40 years) were spent working for Nebuchadnezzar, up to the time of his death when Daniel was 58. Daniel was 67 when Belshazzar became co-regent and 81 when he was overthrown 14 years later. Daniel had his vision of the Ancient of Days in Belshazzar's first year[27] (Dan. 7:1) and his vision of the four kingdoms two years later (Dan. 8:1). Thus Daniel got his understanding of the wider context of God's strategy in his late 60s, when the Babylonian Empire had just over ten years to go.

Darius the Mede came to the throne in 539 BC[28] and the Persian Cyrus took over in 538 BC. Daniel was probably thrown into the lion's den (Dan. 6) that year. In 538 BC Cyrus issued a decree or edict allowing the Jews to return to Jerusalem. The third year of Cyrus, 536 BC, was when 'a word is revealed to Daniel' (Dan. 10:1).

Daniel was promoted to high office, 'ruler over the whole province of Babylon, and chief prefect over all the wise men' (Dan. 2:48), very early in his life. Most unusually he remained effectively as First Civil Servant, or Senior Permanent Secretary, for most of his career. He was clearly efficient ('no ground for complaint', Dan. 6:4), wise (1:4) and understanding. He was a spiritual man, a man of regular prayer (2:18, 6:10). His Jewish values remained with him all his life ('no ... corruption', 6:4, NRSV). He was a man of principle, which greatly irritated his colleagues, since it showed them in a bad light, and was willing on more than one occasion to risk all (1:12, 6:10). He was good in relationships, not only with his three companions (2:49), but also in what was obviously a strong and warm working relationship with King Nebuchadnezzar, which lasted for 40-plus years.

During the bulk of his reign, Nebuchadnezzar was not in expansionist mood; his father had effectively built the Babylonian Empire. He was primarily an Emperor of consolidation, and Daniel helped him to do this *par excellence*. Nebuchadnezzar had no visions of becoming anything other than great in his own eyes. After his death, and the turbulent years of his successors, Daniel was able to see the bigger picture and could thus put the whole Babylonian Empire into its historical context of the first of four Empires: Babylon, Medo-Persia, Greece and Rome. He was aware of a larger, broader strategy that God was shaping across these different Empires and thus was able to interpret the lesser strategies of Babylon within that framework.

Visions come for various reasons; they include enlarging 'our understanding of current events' and showing 'the promised future'.[29] Both of these were true of Daniel. He continually practised the values he had gained from his childhood at home in Jerusalem. He was strengthened to go on keeping them partly by his working circumstances but especially in the light of the future he knew God was making. He knew what was important to do, and did it. In terms of our understanding of vision, though, Daniel, like John in the Book of Revelation, did not himself understand (any more than we do) the full import of the specific visions entrusted to him.

Three wise men

Moses, Hezekiah and Daniel. Priest-maker, king and prophet. Pre-settlement, the monarchy and exile. A politician, a king and a civil servant. Forty-, thirty- and sixty-plus years in leadership. Foundational, religious and prophetic. Futuristic, military and relational. In Belbin's terminology,[30] a shaper, a shaper and a director. All strategic leaders.

Three wise men from the many that could have been chosen from the pages of Scripture. Why choose these in a book about strategic thinking? Because, in their own way, they all thought strategically. They did not think identically, however. Christian leaders today, even those with similar responsibilities, will not necessarily think alike and you may find yourself drawn more to one of these biblical biographies than the others.

Moses

Moses is important as an example of strategic thinking not only because in one sense he was the father of the Jewish nation but also because 'he endured as seeing him who is invisible' (Heb. 11:27). He accepted his position as leader because of the special call that God made on his life when he was 80 years old. However, he also personally affirmed the long-term goal that he knew the Lord was about. He knew the hurly-burly of slavery and the effect it had had on the lives and attitudes of the people of Israel: the depths of day-to-day survival, a forgetfulness of their history and a despair about the promises made to Abraham, Isaac and Jacob. Moses knew his main work was to be one of transformation, which would require dogged determination and strict adherence to long-term objectives (taking the people to the Promised Land of milk and honey).

Chapter 5 describes what BHAGs are. Moses had one! It was to make a rabble into a nation fit for an inheritance. He would never have dreamt of calling it Horizon Mission Methodology, but in effect that is what it was. A huge distant goal towards which he was marching, and in the process enabling people to build the structures that would be necessary for what was invisible for the majority but which he could clearly see. What he learned from Jethro about the importance of delegation (Ex. 18) gave him the relational tools he needed for his task. Brueggemann puts it in a fascinating way: he had 'the task of reframing [which] is supplanting amnesia with memory and supplanting despair with hope'.[31] Moses was sustained in that long process because he 'saw' Christ who would be the ultimate fulfilment of God's promise to Israel and all for which Moses was working.

Hezekiah

Of Hezekiah it might be said, as Bacon said of Henry VII, that 'what he minded he compassed'. He had a clear objective, an orderly mind and the authority with which to accomplish it. Granted an extension mid-term, as it were, by the Lord he had twice the opportunity to make the changes he felt so strongly about. He worked what we will later call the Military Model – he knew what he wanted to do and how to do it. His partial success, though, was mitigated because his son's activities negated much of what he had done. Was Hezekiah so involved in national affairs that he had no time for his family? Was this critical lack of applying priorities the principal reason for subsequent failure? It may well have been a contributing factor. Sadly, the faith and commitment of even the most godly of parents may be rejected by their children, though in God's sovereignty He may use others to fulfil His purposes.

However, for the Military Model to succeed there has to be a further agenda, a hidden agenda, which might be thought of as the invisible focus. A 'Centre of Gravity' is needed, that is, a key event to be successfully undertaken, or a new climate to be generated, or a new-found willingness to co-operate by key people, which when fulfilled will allow the overt actions to be acceptable. Either Hezekiah didn't realise this need, or he failed to achieve it. This was the main reason for disaster after his reign. Perhaps it is the key difference between him and his grandson, Josiah, of whom it was said 'there was no king like him' (2 Kgs.

23:25). Was the restarting of the celebration of Passover the 'Centre of Gravity' for Josiah, or the finding of the Book of the Law (2 Kgs. 22:8)?

Åsne Seierstad is a bookseller in Kabul, Afghanistan, and was there through the Taliban regime and its dismantling by the Americans in 2002. She is a sharp observer of the Afghan scene. In her book[32] she writes:

> Afghanistan has a new government, and women can go to school and to universities. But if they have a father or brother who says, 'No, you cannot go to school, you cannot take off your burka,' it doesn't matter. There are parts of Afghanistan where people didn't notice when the Taliban came or went, because the women never went outside anyway. It shows why change takes such a long time. It doesn't help just to change the government. You have to change every father, grandfather, cousin and brother.

For Hezekiah (and many others later) to be successful, he would have had to change 'every father, grandfather, cousin and brother', an unachievable task in his lifespan.

Daniel

Daniel was a senior civil servant for over 60 years, two-thirds of which were served under a megalomaniac Emperor to whom he faithfully witnessed of the one true God. That Emperor, Nebuchadnezzar, came to acknowledge, bless and honour Daniel's God 'for His dominion is an everlasting dominion' (Dan. 4:34). Daniel was the efficient administrator who gave Nebuchadnezzar's visions to others to fulfil, the archetype of the Relating and Delegating model described in Chapter 6.

The last third of his career, however, was turbulent, with emperors coming and going at regular (and short!)

intervals. God then provided Daniel with visions and understanding of the broad overall political picture of the next 400 years or so, which Daniel used as opportunity afforded. Daniel's vision, however, was not in the visions and their interpretation but beyond even these – to the Ancient of Days (7:13). He was able to distinguish crises from ordinary actions; he could see the end from the beginning.

Effectively this gave Daniel a total confidence and assurance so that he could face the king and all his assembled lords with his explanations of the writing on the wall. He knew that the interpretation he gave was correct and he was able to use that to tell the assembled rulers that God abominates pride and arrogance and will bring them down. When the new Empire was founded (with the supreme test of being thrown to the lions), Daniel was once again appointed as the key strategist. His relational authority was despised but faced by a supreme challenge Daniel did not falter: 'Before you, O king, I have done no wrong' (Dan. 6:22). His values and principles remained constant even when circumstances changed very greatly.

Thus, three wise men, who were all strategic leaders in their time. They accomplished much, not always with success. Strategic thinking is not a password for victory. They did not find their calling easy, but probably found their experience of action very fulfilling. What, then, are the modes of strategic thinking they exhibited? The rest of this book explains.

Notes

1 Oswald Sanders, *Spiritual Leadership* (London: Marshall, Morgan & Scott, 1967), p. 50.
2 Walter Brueggemann, *The Prophetic Imagination* (Minneapolis: Fortress Press, 1978), p. 36 ff.
3 Thomas Edwards, *The Epistle to the Hebrews* (London: Hodder & Stoughton, 1889), p. 253.
4 Moshe Greenberg, *Understanding Exodus* (New York: Behrman House, 1969), p. 71.
5 F.B. Meyer, *Exodus* (Religious Tract Society, 1911), p. 65.
6 Terence Fretheim, *Exodus Interpretation* (Louisville, Kentucky: John Knox Press, 1991), p. 54.
7 R. Kent Hughes, *Hebrews Volume 2: An Anchor for the Soul* (Illinois: Crossway, 1993), p. 121.
8 Ibid.
9 William Lane, *Hebrews 9–13*, Word Biblical Commentary (Dallas, Texas: Word, 1991), p. 376.
10 Brueggemann, *The Prophetic Imagination*, p. 13.
11 Ibid.
12 Ibid., pp. 66, 67 and 111 respectively.
13 Hans Wildberger, *Isaiah 1–12: A Commentary* (Minneapolis: Fortress Press, 1991), p. 248.
14 John Oswalt, *New International Commentary on the Old Testament: Isaiah 1–39*, R.K. Harrison (general ed.) (Grand Rapids, Michigan: Eerdmanns, 1988), p. 189.
15 Michael Wilcock, *The Message of Chronicles: One Church, One Faith, One Lord*, The Bible Speaks Today (Leicester: IVP, 1987), p. 244.
16 Martin J. Selman, *2 Chronicles: A Commentary*, Tyndale Old Testament Commentary (Leicester: IVP, 1994), p. 488.
17 Richard Platt, *1 & 2 Chronicles*, Mentor Commentary (Ross-shire: Christian Focus, 1998), p. 424.
18 Wilcock, *The Message of Chronicles*, p. 247.
19 Ibid., p. 244.
20 J.A. Thompson, *1, 2 Chronicles*, New American Commentary (Nashville: Broadman & Holman, 1994), p. 345.
21 Wilcock, *The Message of Chronicles*, p.243.

[22] John Collin, *Daniel* (Minneapolis: Fortress Press, 1993), p. 130.

[23] Stephen Miller, *Daniel*, New American Commentary (Nashville: Broadman & Holman, 1994), p. 56, following D. J. Wiseman, *Chronicles of Chaldean Kings* (London: The Trustees of the British Museum, 1961), p. 25.

[24] Miller, *Daniel*, p. 240.

[25] Ibid., p. 151 for this date.

[26] Ibid., interpreting Daniel 7, so that Belshazzar's third year (Dan. 8) would be in 550 BC.

[27] Taking the year of succession as the first year of the reign (as per E.S. Young, *The Prophecy of Daniel* [Grand Rapids, Michigan: Eerdmanns, 1966], p. 269).

[28] Miller writes of 'an intense spiritual conflict (which) took place during the first year of Darius the Mede' (*Daniel*, p. 289).

[29] Peter Brierley, *Vision Building* (London: Hodder & Stoughton, 1989 and London: Christian Research, 1994), p. 97.

[30] Meredith Belbin, *Management Teams: Why they Succeed or Fail* (London: Butterworth-Heinemann, 1981, and most years since!).

[31] Brueggemann, *The Prophetic Imagination*, p. 49.

[32] Åsne Seierstad, *The Bookseller of Kabul* (London: Little & Brown, 2003).

Chapter 4

♣ Vision Building

Clubs are an effective but blunt instrument. As weapons they can be used for dreadful and often fatal purposes, as a horrific biography of one Cambodian refugee testifies[1] (the story is in the notes at the end of the chapter). Clubs are used in many sports, whether as golf clubs, polo-sticks, croquet mallets or cricket bats. In golf, for example, the club is used to hit a ball in the direction you want it to go. Clubs are also meeting places, where groups of people can discuss and agree courses of action, enjoy activities, and so on.

So a 'club' is the appropriate symbol from a pack of cards to be linked with this particular method of strategic thinking, which is a blunt way of moving forwards, aided by a team of supporters or a parish congregation.

What is Vision Building?

Vision Building is the name given to a simple, almost mechanical, way of thinking future, which has been successfully used by hundreds of churches, businesses and organisations. It has been described in detail from a Christian perspective in a book of that title;[2] this chapter summarises and applies the relevant points from that volume.

'Vision Building' is about *building a vision*, that is, it is looking forwards, seeing ahead to a new or different situation. A seesaw without a balance in the middle would just be a flat plank; with a fulcrum, however, it becomes great fun for children. Likewise, your vision is the vital fulcrum that holds strategy and guiding principles together. The principles give the framework for the endeavour, the vision gives the future picture and the strategy is the way of fulfilling it. The Ten Commandments were the principles (or some of them); the 'land flowing with milk and honey' was the vision; the conquering settlement of the tribes of Israel the fulfilment. The vision was central and crucial; without it the Israelites would never have got there.

Visions have a number of features:

- They are *personal*, that is, they usually come to just one individual who then shares it with others. Virtually all the visions in the Scriptures come to a single person, the prime mover.

- They are *clear*. The vision can be talked about. It is specific. People know what it is you are hoping to do. In the 1980s my brother's vision was 'to buy a narrowboat so that the less privileged children of Lewisham could have the opportunity of a holiday and see the countryside'. Everyone knew what he meant. He achieved it with much hard work, eventually seeing three narrowboats commissioned.

- They are *shareable*. The vision may come to an individual but it must be shared with others. For leaders to be followed, their vision must be communicated.

- They are *realistic*. A vision invariably builds upon and uses your gifts. God builds on our previous experience of walking with Him, and our past understanding of Him, and then moves us on to new levels of revelation.

- They are *beyond oneself.* Christians especially need to think globally. 'For God so loved the *world* that He gave His one and only Son' John (3:16) tells us. 'Vision is a confidence of the infinite possibilities for the people of God,' said a former Archbishop of Canterbury.[3]

- They are *energising.* Energy motivates. Nothing significant for God was ever accomplished without energy. David Wilkerson, founding pastor of the Times Square Church in New York, said one Sunday in June 2003 in his sermon, 'I'm 72, and I have energy,' and went on to call for 100 under-25-year-old volunteers to go overseas with the message of Christ. Several hundred responded.[4]

- They are *humbling.* Paul makes some astounding statements in Ephesians. God created Adam and Eve, yet planned from eternity (3:11) the work of Christ, implying He knew they would fall. However many generations there have been between Adam and Eve and the beginning of the 21st century, the Lord knew the total genealogy so well that *before* the foundation of the world He chose *us* in Christ (1:4). He knew me before I was born – and before my great-great-great grandfather was born too! If that is not sufficient He also knew what He could do with my life, for 'we are His workmanship, created in Christ Jesus for good works, which God prepared beforehand, that we should walk in them' (2:10). Such knowledge is 'too wonderful for me' (Job 42:3). God is working His purposes out as year succeeds to year, but He is doing this not just in the macro, but in the micro of my life, my destiny, my actions. Any God-given vision should result from the visionary being a humble follower of the Lord. 'All that I am, He made me; All that I have, He gave me,' went an old chorus, 'And all that ever I hope to be, Jesus alone must do for me.'

Organisational vision

The structure of vision

A vision of this type requires a context for its *formation* as well as a context or framework for its *fulfilment*. It is this context, or structure, which effectively makes and identifies this method of strategic thinking; the other methods do not require this. There is a logic about it, which is why those who like detail and getting things worked out and completed find this method of thinking satisfying. This logic may be expressed as shown[5] in Table 4.1, in which the 'fulcrum' nature of vision between principles and strategy may be clearly seen.

The Will, Word and Work of God reflect God's sovereignty. He is over all. Nothing happens without His acquiescence or Will, though He is not the cause of evil, nor the originator of temptation. The Word of God is the Son of God who came to redeem the world and by His death made a once-for-all sacrifice enabling salvation to be offered to all. The Work of God is undertaken today through the Holy Spirit, who convicts the world of sin, righteousness and Judgement, and who indwells every believer so each may display the fruit of the Spirit. The Will, Word and Work of God thus reflect the Trinity of God the Father, God the Son and God the Spirit, whose key purpose is to further the Kingdom of God. Such overriding control and sovereignty is above all our searching for vision, and desire for service.

The next words, Purpose, Mission, Vision and Thrusts, will be described in more detail shortly. Three of the final words, Goals, Priorities, Plans and Action, are more properly the domain of a time management course,[6] and those interested in working these through should consider attending one of these.[7] However, goals and priorities are discussed briefly in Chapter 7, and planning is described later in this chapter.

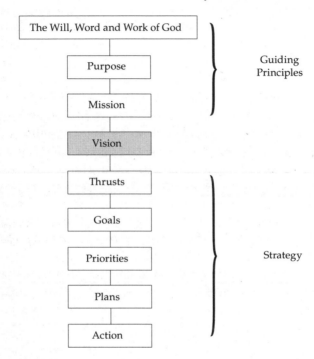

Figure 4.1
The structure of vision

Four questions

This method of thinking strategically focuses around four questions, each relating to a word in Figure 4.1, which thus imposes a structure on them:

Purpose	→	Why are you here?
Mission	→	What are you doing?
Vision	→	What will you become?
Thrusts	→	How will you do it?

The first three of these questions are time related. The first, purpose, looks to the past. The second, mission, looks to the present. The third, vision, looks to the future. This method of strategic thinking recognises where you have come from, in order to work out where you hope to go. These four questions are now considered in more detail.

Purpose: Why are you here?

Where you have come from can be important for your future. Never dismiss the traditions you inherit; sometimes they can be very significant. A church founded to serve deaf people, for example, will probably always see that as its prime ministry; the original purpose continues into the future even if the method by which it may be undertaken greatly changes.

Answering the question 'Why are you here?' or 'Why was your church started?' is usually fairly easy. Here are three purpose statements deliberately taken from the *Tyne and Wear Christian Directory*, which was published in 1986,[8] to show, like most purpose statements, that they haven't changed across the subsequent years:

> *Christ Church, Gateshead:* Anglican presence in the inner city.

> *St Agnes Roman Catholic Church, Gateshead:* To serve the spiritual needs of the parishioners in Crawcrook and surrounding areas.

> *Whitburn Methodist, South Tyneside:* A village chapel forming a nucleus for wider sharing.

This is not to say that purpose statements never change, but if they do it is likely to be after a considerable time, perhaps 50 or 100 years. Nor are the statements given above in order for them to be critiqued; they are the words of the minister who answered the question at the time. They each make a statement about their church, and each, as it happens, is very different – a presence, a service and a nucleus. Each will bring with them their own context for working out that purpose, and their own culture also. The outworking will change over time, and so probably the culture, but, if the church wishes, the purpose remains supreme.

Should at some stage a new minister feel that the reason for Christ Church's existence was, in the words of the St Agnes' priest, 'to serve the spiritual needs of the parishioners', he/she could so restate Christ Church's purpose. To have any effect in practice, however, it would also require a total rethink of how best those needs might be met – in other words, fresh strategic thinking. Thus past purpose can impact future vision, but usually only through a re-evaluation. Such perhaps can be undertaken more easily for churches or other bodies where such statements are rarely written down.

Organisations, agencies and businesses may well print their purpose. Three examples, publicly available from the stated organisations, are:

Institute of Management: To promote the development and successful exercise of management skills.

Crusaders: To release an army of radical young people who are committed to taking the Gospel to the generations who don't know Jesus Christ.

Mothers' Union: To be specially concerned with all that strengthens and preserves marriage and Christian family life.

All begin with 'to'
Many purpose statements begin with an infinitive, that is, a verb beginning with the word 'to'. An infinitive states a purpose without involving people in the definition of that purpose, even if people are essential for its fulfilment. This means that such statements are crisp, detached and have, well, a sense of purpose!

Why do you exist?
This is a close but a sufficiently different alternative question to arrive at a similar answer. There is no implicit locational element in this question. Charles Handy, the management guru, suggests using this to identify purpose. He gives some examples from well-known companies:

> **Walt Disney:** To make people happy.
>
> **Wal-Mart:** To give ordinary folk the chance to buy the same things as rich people.
>
> **Merck:** To preserve and improve human life.
>
> **Sony:** To experience the joy of advancing and applying technology for the benefit of the public.

These statements can be made to fit changing circumstances. For example, your church may have been started 'to fulfil a need on a new estate'. Over time the estate will no longer be new and the needs will be different, but the original purpose remains true.

How to identify your purpose
In practice, how does your church or organisation work out its purpose?

- Have a discussion amongst the senior leadership team and ask each member to write down his/her answer to the question 'Why are we here?' or 'Why do we exist?'

- Then compare answers. What are the elements the members have in common? See if you can formulate a statement, beginning with the word 'to', from those areas where you agree. That may be sufficient, but you may wish to add another phrase or clause or adjective.

- In what respects are your answers different? Are these differences important? Should any be incorporated into your statement? If you jointly feel any should, try and do so, with agreement.

- When you have a finished statement, share it with others and note their reactions. If necessary, make further changes.

- Come back to the whole thing in six months' time and make further adjustments to the wording or the concepts. Then put it on your letterhead or magazine or in any other public way.

There are times when to know why an organisation exists is essential. On one occasion I was asked to lead a 'Vision Building' day for a well-known Christian organisation. As part of the process I split the executive leadership team (about 12 people) into two groups and asked each to write down what the purpose of the organisation was, expecting to get two broadly similar statements with different wording. We would then jointly agree a combined statement. To my surprise, and theirs, they came up with two different and contradictory statements! We spent the next two hours trying to work out which statement, or which new statement, really did reflect that organisation's *raison d'être*. Unless you know what you are here for, it's a bit difficult trying to achieve it!

Mission: What are you doing?

Mission relates to the here-and-now environment. It is focused on the present activities of the business, agency or church. It answers the question of 'how?' the purpose is being fulfilled, or hopes to be fulfilled; it is sometimes taken as the key objective statement.

Thus, for example, the mission statement of Christian Research is: 'Giving Christian leaders the insights and skills required for strategic planning.' All its activities, including research, training, consultancy, publishing and membership activities, come within this broad rubric.

Two organisations may have a similar purpose but differing missions. Thus Oxfam and Christian Aid both have as their purpose the alleviation of suffering through relief and development world-wide. Oxfam deals with this largely in a participative manner (by organising actions at local level, bringing in extra staff and resources as necessary) whereas Christian Aid handles its work mostly in a non-participative manner by providing resources (usually finance) to organisations already in a position in a country to handle the needs.

A single organisation may have more than one distinct mission, like **Statistics Finland**, the National Statistics Office of Finland, whose mission is:

1) Helping citizens form a reliable picture of society,

2) Aiding Government and corporate decision making, and

3) Creating conditions for social and economic research.[9]

Crusaders also has a double mission:

1) Reaching young people for Jesus Christ,

2) Engaging them in effective Christian living.[10]

The Diocese of Rochester has a multiple mission statement as well. It 'seeks, in the power of the Holy Spirit, to confess Jesus Christ as Lord and to proclaim the Word and Work of God so that humanity is redeemed, community restored and creation renewed'. It does this by:

1) Enabling people to worship God so that they may serve Him faithfully,

2) Equipping people to learn more of Christ from God's Word and God's World,

3) Encouraging people to witness boldly to what He is doing in their lives,

4) Engaging with people in the work of justice, compassion and healing.[11]

All end in '-ing'

Mission statements all explain what the organisation or church is doing NOW, that is to say, they need to be phrased in the present. One way of ensuring this is to phrase them so that the first word is a verb that ends in '-ing'. The above examples all do this. Here are three others, all examples from churches:

Ebenezer Church, Tyneside [Christian Brethren]: Providing regular family worship, Bible-based teaching and preaching of the Gospel.

Christ Church, Bromley [Anglican]: Making Jesus known.

URC Church, North London: Providing a centre for worship, and facilities for the local community.

Testing your statement

Management Futures is a forward-looking business dedicated to giving the best counselling and management training, using 21st-century techniques. Its two founding directors were both BBC Heads of Department. It suggests that mission statements should get positive answers to the following questions:

- Is it short and simple?
- Is it inspiring?
- Does it describe what you uniquely do?
- Could your staff [or congregation] say what it is?
- Could your most junior staff [or newcomers] say what it is?
- Are you using it to measure your performance?
- Have you revisited it in the last two years?[12]

Not all the above examples would get seven positive answers to these questions! They add, however, at least two concepts that can aid the process of identifying the mission of your church or organisation. One of these is 'uniqueness'. While that may not mean something that you and you only do, it can well mean something that you are particularly known for, have specialised in, have a particular professional ability for, or something else which when people hear the name of your church or organisation say, 'Ah yes, that's the group that ... ' One church was particularly well known for conducting 'good funerals', but decided not to put that in its mission statement!

The second element in these questions is using the mission statement as something by which to measure performance. That assumes the statement can be readily used in this way. 'Making Jesus known', for example, would not readily yield to a measurable criterion – the size of the congregation? the number of activities involving the community? the number of evangelistic addresses?

However, it should be used to ensure that in every discussion or planning meeting the question is asked, 'How does this help us meet our mission statement?'

Vision: What will you become?

This is the element that looks to the future. What is it that you want to become? Where are you going? Or, if those are too vague, what will you have become in, say, ten years' time? (The number ten is completely variable, but the period should probably be for at least three years ahead.)

This is where the comment made in Chapter 1 is relevant – not everyone can answer such questions, or even know how to answer them. Perhaps a third of people can think in this way. Hence the need for a small, compact team of people able to work together in the senior leadership group.

One of Solomon's Proverbs is unambiguous – 'Where there is no vision the people perish' (Prov. 29:18, AV). The way different translations of the Bible handle this verse is illuminating. 'People break loose without a guiding hand' (Moffatt). 'Where there is no vision, the people get out of hand' (Jerusalem). 'Where there is no revelation, the people cast off restraint' (RAV and NIV). 'Where there is no prophecy, the people cast off restraint' (NRSV). 'Where there is no one in authority, the people break loose' (NEB). 'A nation without God's guidance is a nation without order' (GNB). 'When people do not accept divine guidance, they run wild' (New Living Bible). 'Without guidance from God law and order disappear' (CEV).

Two of the alternative words used for vision in these translations, revelation and prophecy, are used elsewhere in the Scriptures to translate the same Hebrew word. The need for help, clear leadership, firm understanding, comes through. Without vision, however, it is not only the people who will perish. Without vision, society perishes. Without vision, the church perishes. Without vision, the parachurch agency perishes. Without vision, leadership perishes. Without vision, you and I perish. Vision is not an optional extra: it is essential. As blind and deaf Helen Keller once said, 'There is only one thing worse than being blind ... being able to see, but having no vision.'

Vision must be future related

What is vision? At its simplest it is a statement about the future. The travel guide firm Frommer's ran a good series of advertisements in the mid-1990s. 'Know where you're going before you get there' was their strap line,[13] and they expected you to buy their guide to Nepal, say, before your visit. The assumption was that you knew you were aiming to go to Nepal, not just 'going somewhere on holiday'. However, the punchline could also relate to time generally, and might be translated, 'Know your vision so that you can state where you are headed.'

'Vision', says George Verwer, who began the mission literature agency Operation Mobilisation in 1964 and has seen it grow world wide since, 'is a powerful sense of what needs to be done and the initiative to take hold of it and work towards its completion.'[14]

Determining your vision, or the vision of your church or organisation, means thinking ahead. What will be different as a consequence of your work in, say, 2015? What will you have achieved by the time you retire? How will you be regarded by the next generation of Christian leadership? What epitaph would you like put on your tombstone? These are tough questions, not easily or quickly answered.

Some say vision has to be inspiring, challenging, creative, revealed. It certainly helps if it is! But I am not sure that it *has* to be such. In terms of club-like strategic thinking, vision is a firm, future destination to which both you and your organisation are clearly travelling.

The importance of being future cannot be overstated. One church's statement was 'To help people recognise the presence of God in their daily lives and relationships.' This is a worthy objective, and doubtless challenging. But it is not *vision*; it is a statement of current intentions and activity. It is in fact a *mission* statement and would have been better expressed 'Helping people recognise ...' Be sure your 'vision' has a future implication! This can be expressed:

Purpose + Today's World = Mission

Purpose + Tomorrow's World = Vision[15]

The impact of vision

True visions make a difference! They impact our *world*; we are never quite the same again once we have determined what it is we are aiming to do. They impact our *learning*; we now read certain books, buy relevant videos, go on particular courses. They impact our *resources*; we are now saving to build an extension, send someone to Africa, or collecting clothing to give to needy asylum seekers. They impact our *relationships*; we need to get to know special groups of people, approach certain officials, write to relevant leaders. They can impact our *structures*; if they do, this is usually in radical way – we have to be properly organised so as to deliver the goods. They impact our *image*; we are now seen to be people with a message, a driven group perhaps, but those wanting to make a difference.

Visions can be measurable, but don't have to be

Sometimes they can be *measurable*. Then you will know whether or not you have achieved what you set out to do. Three such church vision statements are:

URC Church, North London: To increase support to young families, so they become 40% of our attendance in five years' time.

Rhema Church, Johannesburg, South Africa: To build a church community of 25,000 in 15 years. [This was stated in 1984, and they had fulfilled it by the mid-1990s, ahead of schedule, so they are now aiming to build a church community of 50,000 by 2010, and have already enlarged the church to seat 8,000 at a single service!]

Emmanuel Church, South West London: By 2000, we will be an attractive, worshipping fellowship ... so that those linked to the church will number about 1,000.

But visions do not have to be directly measurable. They then run the danger of becoming more diffuse, lacking crispness, but that doesn't mean they are incorrect or unworkable. Not at all! Some such vision statements are:

St Andrew's, Eastcote: To so communicate the excitement and joy of the message Jesus taught that people will gladly respond.

Salesian Sisters of St John Bosco: To allow others to capture responsible, caring, challenging and enthusiastic leadership roles.

Handbag.com: To be the most useful online site for women.[16]

Market Research Society: To be an organisation that reflects an exciting and forward-looking industry.[17]

How do we get our vision?

There is no single or simple way. It will probably need to involve many of the following:

- Personal and corporate prayer, asking God for guidance, wisdom and revelation.
- Intensive discussion within the leadership team. This can sometimes be helped using an external facilitator. It means first identifying, and agreeing, the purpose of the organisation and its present mission. This method of strategic thinking recognises and values past purposes and current activities. You might need to spend half a day stating, or restating, your purpose and mission.
- Keep the discussion going. Reckon on taking a full day at least! This is not an activity over a cup of tea. In the light of why you exist and what you are doing, what are you likely to become in, say, five years' time? Ask people to write the answer down on a post-it note, then put them all up and read what each has said. What are the common threads? You may well be able to identify three, five, even more items of importance.
- Then comes the crucial part. Imagine yourself in a helicopter looking down on these five or so items. Can you find a wider yet specific statement that embraces either them all or the majority? Are some included within others if certain ones are adopted? Go for a wider context, a broader view, an overarching formulary. This can take time, and you may need to return to it on a future occasion, but getting this far is a huge help. It may not mean agreement initially, and this has to be worked through. No one said strategic thinking was easy! But it is out of such deep yearnings and struggles that the vision comes.

And then what? For nearly 30 years, till it was taken out of service in October 2003, Concorde sped between New York and London in three-and-a quarter hours at a speed of Mach Two, twice the speed of sound. To do that its throttle was always fully open. Concorde constantly flew flat out! So must we, once our vision is known.

Personal vision

Much of the above relates specifically to forming a vision for a business, agency, parachurch organisation, a church or other like corporate body. But it may be that you need to know your personal vision. Unless you know where you yourself are going, what (as mentioned above) you would like to see as an epitaph on your tombstone, how can you lead others into the future? In John Naisbitt's second major book, *Re-inventing the Corporation*,[18] he quotes Buck Blessing, a career consultant, who says, 'The most difficult person to manage is the person who has no idea what he or she wants to do.'

What we want to do comes to us in various ways. In the 21st century, our childhood experience can be crucial, especially if our parents separated. If we marry, our partner becomes a critical piece of the jigsaw. If we are Christian, prayer, reading the Bible and our church will be important. We may experience dreams, though these may not be immediately understood. Our understanding of life and our life story to date will need to be noted. External information can be useful. Understanding our giftings is essential. Knowing our skills is important too, and they are not the same as our gifts. Gifts are given to us, 'the pack of cards dealt to us at birth', as someone once put it. Skills are the abilities we develop by learning, whether that is generally through experience or on a specific training programme.

There are some interesting life summaries in the Bible:

- Enoch walked with God (Gen. 5:24)

- Moses, whom the Lord knew face to face (Deut. 34:10)

- Saul and Jonathan, beloved and lovely! (2 Sam. 1:23)

- Before him [Josiah], there was no king like him (2 Kgs. 23:25)
- Jehoram ... departed with no one's regret (2 Chron. 21:20)
- Abraham, my friend (Is. 41:8)
- Antipas, my witness, my faithful one (Rev. 2:13)

There are about 80,000 verbs in the English language. If you could choose one to put on your tombstone, what would it be? He preached, she loved, he cared, she laboured, he counted for God, he enabled, he remained faithful, she understood, he built ... ?

Such vision is stimulating. We need people today like William Leech of Newcastle who, almost a century ago, said he wanted to do three things in his life – be a successful businessman, own a Rolls Royce and give large amounts of money to charity. All three were fulfilled and he donated many, many millions of pounds, mostly to five particular charities. The *Manchester Guardian* on 3rd July 1938 urged the Prime Minister, Neville Chamberlain, to use Winston Churchill's gifts 'in any capacity', putting patriotism above personal rancour, because England needed 'Ministers of vision'.[19]

Such vision is empowering. The Longfellow verse is still relevant:

> Lives of great men all remind us
> We can make our lives sublime.
> And, departing, leave behind us
> Footprints on the sands of time.

Such sentiments are appealing, but can be dangerous for Christians. The Psalmist reminds us 'Not unto us, O Lord, not unto us, but unto Thy name give glory' (115:1 AV). We must constantly remember that the purpose of a vision for a Christian is not self-aggrandisement or boasting, but the glory of God.

Ultimately, a vision has to be followed through. Benjamin Disraeli once said, 'The secret of success is constancy of purpose.' We're back to Concorde again – keeping on keeping on going!

Thrusts

We began this chapter with four questions. The fourth was 'Thrusts ➔ How will you do it?' and to this we now turn. Thrusts are the key areas through which the vision will be fulfilled. They are the centres of energy, or the departments to be used. They are the key pivots around which everything else will hang. However, the outworking of each thrust requires careful planning.

How do you plan the outworking of your vision? With the knowledge it may not work out as expected! 'We make our own plans, but the Lord decides where we will go' (Prov. 16:9) – and it may not be where we anticipate!

There are two broad considerations in any planning exercise. Firstly, is this a one-off item, or is a whole series of things to be planned? Secondly, is this a fairly simple operation, or is it complex? These may be summed up as follows, where one or more thrusts may be in any box:

Table 4.2
Different ways to plan

No \ Dfy	Simple	Complex
Single	*Portcullis*	*Business*
Multiple	*Scenario*	PERT

Dfy = Difficulty

We will look briefly at portcullis[20] and business[21] planning, where basically a single item or thrust is being planned. Scenario[22] planning is essentially a replication of portcullis or business planning when the additional question 'What if?' is thrown into the arena. What if inflation quadruples in the next year? What if the Prime Minister is assassinated? What if incitement to religious hatred increases sharply? What if Christian organisations are compelled to accept employment practices they feel undermine their ethos? What if our building is burnt down? Charities now have to have a 'risk assessment' as part of their annual audit; scenario planning takes these risks one by one and works out in detail what the appropriate response should be.

PERT,[23] which stands for Programme Evaluation and Review Technique, is but one example of many programmes available. All such programmes are sophisticated planning mechanisms involving flow charts and the like. They are necessary when building a block of flats, for example, to ensure that the foundation is built before the bricks for the walls arrive, and that the roof is on before the electricians start wiring. Today such planning is handled through their laptops by specialists. If readers of this book ever feel they need this kind of planning, don't even think about attempting it – just go to an expert!

Portcullis planning

Planning ultimately is to do with goals. Unless you know what you want to do, or where you are going, you cannot realistically plan how to get there. So the first assumption behind any plan is that you have a goal to plan for. Your thrust, if you like, is identified. The fulfilment of your vision may require several goals to be met, but the process for each is the same.

Plans need to be communicated and the portcullis process allows that very easily. Plans are not architects' blueprints that have to slavishly followed; they are an arrow indicating the intentions one has to get something done.

Portcullis planning requires four prior items before the planning process can begin:

1) A knowledge of what has to be accomplished – the goal, how we want things to be in, say, five years' time.

2) An indication of how things are at the moment (this is the easiest bit!).

3) Those things that are moving in your favour, the support you have, where the wind is behind you.

4) Those things that are moving against you, where the opposition may be seen, where the wind is blowing towards you, making progress hard.

Examples of the first two items are:

- An Anglican church in north Wales: Currently has just two young families in the congregation (four adults aged 25 to 40). Aiming for 20 young families in five years' time.

- Bereavement organisation, Cruise: No branch in a particular town, but aims to establish one in eight months' time.

- Baptist church deacon's prayers for congregation: Haphazard way of praying for friends, family and congregation. Wants to create a daily prayer list of people by end of next week.

- Frustrated lay people want to do more: Currently only one lay person is allowed to read the lesson; laity can take the collection and sing in the choir but do nothing else. By end of the year they want more of the laity reading the lessons, and frequently to lead the prayers.

- Home groups in a Finnish church: Only occasional meetings in homes now, but within 12 months wants to set up regular home fellowships meeting for four months or more each year, subject to weather conditions.

These examples, all based on actual seminar experiences, show how versatile this particular method of planning can be, from small and personal to wider scale and longer term.

To illustrate this process, let me take another example from a seminar. A young Pentecostal pastor in a small, overcrowded church wanted to see a new church built in three years' time. These two elements are inserted in a grid, like the one below, which very vaguely looks like a portcullis (if you have a good imagination!), hence the name. In most tables, entries are made from left to right, but not in this one! Here you start at the right and then fill in the others from the left.

Table 4.3
Example of a portcullis grid

The Present	Helps	Hindrances	Plans	The Goal
Overcrowded small building				Build new church in three years' time

To this are now added the 'helps' and 'hindrances', the positive things that the pastor felt were working in his favour and the negatives that somehow had to be overcome.

Table 4.4
A portcullis grid nearing completion

The Present	Helps	Hindrances	Plans	The Goal
Overcrowded small building	*People:* 1) Were anxious to change 2) Young congregation with practical skills	*People:* 1) No vision 2) Strongly traditional Sunday worship 3) Do not perceive need or opportunity		Build new church in three years' time
	Finance: 1) Land was available 2) £200,000 in building fund	*Finance:* 1) Building fund not large enough 2) Denomination cannot fund		
	Other aids: 1) Good local builders 2) Denomination could give advice	*Other problems:* 1) No architect in the church		

This particular pastor was fortunate in having many folk in his congregation who had the necessary bricklaying, electrical, woodworking, plastering and other such practical skills to give very real help in the actual construction. He also found that one of his key assets, people, were also one of his chief liabilities. That is not unusual, but it is important to identify why they were such. They were fixed in their attitude about small details such as service times, which inhibited alternatives such as having two morning services to alleviate the space problem. His other key problem was finance: while £200,000 is a goodly sum for a small church, it is quite insufficient for a new church building.

At this stage you have a grid containing all the crucial elements of a problem. It can therefore be used with other people for solving it. Problem solving implies 'a process by which the learner combines previously learned elements of knowledge, rules, techniques, skills and concepts to provide a solution to a novel situation'.[24] The grid is an ideal way of presenting the issues, using either an overhead projector or PowerPoint. 'What would you do if this were your problem?' I asked the seminar participants, an all-denominational group of ministers. A number of suggestions were made for the 'Plans' column:

- Go to the Christian Resources Exhibition to find details of a suitable architect.
- Ask the church to pray about the matter.
- Present the project imaginatively to church members.
- Establish a fundraising committee.
- Preach a series of sermons on Nehemiah.

Several of these ideas may not have occurred to the Pentecostal minister; this method encourages constructive thinking to facilitate the problem or originate other solutions. The actual solution was interesting: the minister suddenly remembered that the local pub had recently built an extension with a very pleasant layout and finish. So the fourth column was completed with a view to action on this score and with an eye to convincing the congregation of what was about to happen.

Table 4.5
The completed portcullis grid

The Present	Helps	Hindrances	Plans	The Goal
Overcrowded small building	*People:* 1) Were anxious to change 2) Young congregation with practical skills *Finance:* 1) Land was available 2) £200,000 in building fund *Other aids:* 1) Good local builders 2) Denomination could give advice	*People:* 1) No vision 2) Strongly traditional Sunday worship 3) Do not perceive need or opportunity *Finance:* 1) Building fund not large enough 2) Denomination cannot fund *Other problems:* 1) No architect in the church	*Aim to get congregational agreement within 12 months:* 1) Clarify purposes 2) Formulate building plan 3) Build model of new church 4) Educate congregation *Contact local brewery:* Would architect for their recent extension help us?	Build new church in three years' time

The plans also help to identify the thrusts needed to fulfil the project. They might be summarised: Planning, Education, Brewery/Architect from the above, though items like Finance and Communication will almost certainly have to be added as well.

This method of planning is simple and has been used on numerous occasions. It is methodical and logical, and so suits those who think or work this way. It identifies all the key steps to completion of the process. It facilitates the completion of each stage. It is easy to use with teams, and thus helps younger people who especially like working this way. It is helpful to communicate the issues for problem solving. It is compact for simple presentation. It allows others to help in problem solving.

However, the method is not perfect! The interrelations of times for each step are not obvious. It is sometimes too succinct. If you have several goals, a separate sheet is required for each. Notwithstanding this, the portcullis grid is recommended as an ideal way for planning one-off and relatively simple projects.

Business planning

Business planning as presented here relates to the planning of a single project, which is recognised to be complex. Most visions can be broken down into three, four or five thrusts. Six is likely to be the maximum; if you have more than that, can two be combined? Suppose a particular project has five broad components: Publicity, Finance, Liaison with Government, Local Authority or others, Recruitment of personnel and Administration. They may be marked on a diagram like this as items 1, 2, 3, 4 and 5:

Figure 4.6
Planning the vision

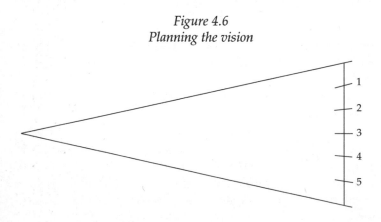

This diagram can help in the planning process. The vision will not be accomplished this year or next year, but we can start moving towards it this year.

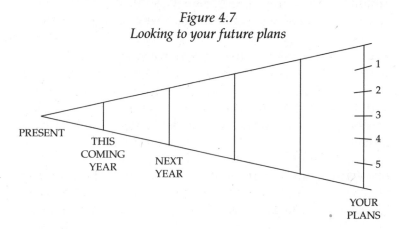

Figure 4.7
Looking to your future plans

Each of your thrusts has some link with the present, if only an indication that more detailed work will be needed on it in time. Represent these links with lines joining your future plans to the present. The diagram then looks like this:

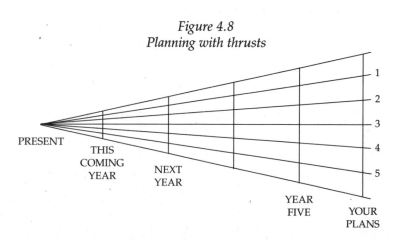

Figure 4.8
Planning with thrusts

Working in this way means that your entire programme is focused on your vision. This is helpful to everyone in the organisation or church. The elements that continue from the past know their place in the future scheme of things; the new elements know their relative position also. Not every thrust lasts for the whole time period, or begins immediately. That does not matter. Keep the line in, even if it represents zero activity when that aspect comes up. One church wanting to hire a music director couldn't afford one, but still had in its budget the heading 'Music Department', under which was the item 'Part-time Director', against which was £0.00. Everyone knew it was there; there was no chance of overlooking it. It was just that its time hadn't come yet.

There is another major value in running your organisation around your key thrusts. In the process of fulfilling your plans, someone may have an idea. 'Wouldn't it be a good idea, pastor, to visit everyone in the area with mince pies to encourage them to come to the carol service?' The pastor may agree, and the idea is added in to the scheme of things. Appropriate time, money and people are allocated.

Someone else, realising that money is a problem, suggests that the minister does a sponsored parachute jump. The minister considers the idea and wonders if the image of parachuting clergy will actually enhance the work. As it does not, he declines, irrespective of his personal preferences for parachutes, which need never be stated! These ideas might be called X and Y and would appear as follows:

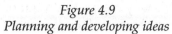

Figure 4.9
Planning and developing ideas

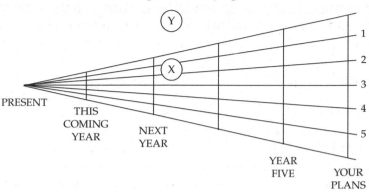

A minister of a large church had a regular meeting with his assistant pastors. Every other week each had to describe publicly what he/she had been doing the past two weeks and what he/she proposed to undertake in the next two weeks. If anybody ever suggested anything out of line with the overall vision, it was prohibited. Any Y activity simply wasn't allowed. In that way, the church not only accomplished their vision, but did so early! Likewise, we need to have the same discipline, and this process gives the scope for that.

The reality, however, is that Figure 4.9 is not an easy diagram from which to construct a business plan, so it needs to be translated into a table, such as given in Table 4.10:

Table 4.10
The kernel of a business plan

Thrust	This year	Next year	The year after	Penulti-mate year	Final year
Publicity	×	×	×	×	×
Finance	×	×	×	×	×
Liaison	×	×	×	×	×
Personnel	×	×	×	×	×
Adminis-tration	×	×	×	×	×

Every × in this table needs to have a statement of activity or measurement associated with it. For a few, it will be zero. But overall in a single span you will have a broad outline of the work to be done to fulfil the vision. Working that out in the detail of Table 4.10 is where the strategic thinking comes in, but when broken down in this way into annual components of each thrust it does not become too difficult.

You may well wish to have some explanatory notes to go with the completed table. Working out how to do any individual × in the table may require a portcullis grid, but the business plan gives an overview of complex activity.

If the time periods suggested – every year – are for any reason not convenient, simply substitute time periods that are more relevant – every three or six months, or perhaps two years at a time. Nor does a business plan have to have the same frequencies across its whole span, so it may be easier to have something for three months' time, then the next six months, and then the next year, for example.

Clubs!

There's a lovely cartoon of Tom Wilson's of a little fellow sitting rather forlornly at one end of a seesaw, with no one else in sight. The little fellow muses, 'There's some things you just can't do by yourself!' It's exactly so with strategic thinking and vision. One man or one woman may have the vision, but its fulfilment requires a church, a company, a battalion, all the workforce, an army, a multitude, to make it happen. Don't think yours is any different. If it is worth accomplishing, it has to be accomplished through others.

This is Vision Building, a club-like method to help you move forward towards a distant objective in the company of others. Golf clubs drive a ball to a distant objective. A match consists of a hole-by-hole approach. Likewise, detailed, strategic, step-by-step thinking can help you accomplish your distant vision.

Notes

[1] Sok Rheaksa Vimm, *The Tears of my Soul* (London: Monarch, 2003). Rheaksa tells the story of his parents' home, when his father was a teacher in Cambodia in the 1970s. The Pol Pot regime made them move out of Phnom Penn into the countryside, where, because of his father's profession, all were eventually sentenced to death. The entire family of ten people was taken into the woods and clubbed to death, each falling into the grave they had been made to dig earlier. Rheaksa was stunned but not killed, crawled out when the murderers had gone, and eventually escaped. Now a Christian, married with one small son, he has returned to Cambodia.

[2] Peter Brierley, *Vision Building* (London: Hodder & Stoughton, 1989 and Christian Research, London, 1994).

[3] Most Revd George Carey preaching at a service in Germany in 1988.

[4] Personal observation, 10.00 a.m. morning service, 29th June 2003.

[5] This was originally outlined in a 1986 MARC Europe seminar, 'Vision Building', by Dr David Cormack, at that time Director of Management Training.

[6] They are, however, described in much more detail in the book *Priorities, Planning and Paperwork* by Peter Brierley (London: MARC Europe, and Speldhurst, Kent: MARC, 1992).

[7] Such are regularly held, for example, by Christian Research, London.

[8] David Longley and Mervyn Spearing (eds), *Tyne and Wear Christian Directory* (London: MARC Europe, 1986).

[9] Published in *Sigma*, the Eurostat Magazine, Summer 1995.

[10] Taken from their 2003 brochure.

[11] Given in the Diocesan monthly newspaper, *Rochester Link*, Vol. 7, No. 9, November 1997.

[12] From Management Future's *Newsletter*, Spring 1996, p. 5.

[13] For example, in an advertisement in *The Bookseller*, January 1994.

[14] George Verwer, *Out of the Comfort Zone* (Carlisle: OM, 2000), p. 58.

[15] David Cormack seminar, 'Vision Building'.

[16] *Sheer Inspiration*, produced for BT by *Management Today*, 2001, p. 11.

[17] MRS News, Issue 11, May–June 2003, Statement by the Chair, Jennie Beck, p. 4.

[18] John Naisbitt, *Re-inventing the Corporation* (London: Guild, 1985), p. 87.

[19] William Manchester, *The Caged Lion* (London: Michael Joseph, 1988), p. 427.

[20] This is described in greater detail in Brierley, *Priorities, Planning and Paperwork*, ch. 3, p. 67.

[21] This is described briefly in Brierley, *Vision Building*, ch. 5, p. 166.

[22] This is described briefly in ibid., ch. 5, p. 155; Brierley, *Priorities, Planning and Paperwork*, ch. 3, p. 99, and as a special case of scenario planning in *Priorities, Planning and Paperwork*, ch. 4, p. 107.

[23] This is described in greater detail in Brierley, *Priorities, Planning and Paperwork*, ch. 3, p. 88.

[24] A. Orton, *Learning Mathematics: Issues, Theory and Classroom Practice* (London: Cassell, 1992), p. 35.

Chapter 5

♦ Horizon Mission Methodology

Diamonds are for ever, went the advertisement. Some people are fortunate enough to dig up jewel-encrusted artefacts from Roman or Egyptian times. The diamonds or gold crowns or whatever they find might be tarnished, but when restored they still sparkle and glitter as much as they ever did. Diamonds are valuable jewels, as men will know if their wife has one in her engagement ring! And it is this aspect of a diamond that is important here. What are things that are valued? What does society value? What do I value? What are Christian values? Horizon Mission Methodology (HMM) builds a mechanism of thinking strategically around our values, rock-hard values like diamonds, which, like the jewel, should stay the same for ever!

Do our values change?

HMM assumes that the values we express in an imagined future scenario are the same as motivate us today. This suggests that our values do not change, but is that true? It is something that has only rarely been measured statistically. The European Values Survey has undertaken important studies across many countries in Europe in 1981, 1990 and 1999. A sample of individuals is interviewed in each country over a two- or three-hour period. In such a long interview many questions are asked. The answers are sometimes then merged together to generate a new, composite, variable. One of those was on the topic of 'permissiveness', essentially people's attitudes to sexual morality. Figure 5.1 shows the permissiveness score by age group for the 1981 and 1990 surveys.

Figure 5.1
Degree of permissiveness by age

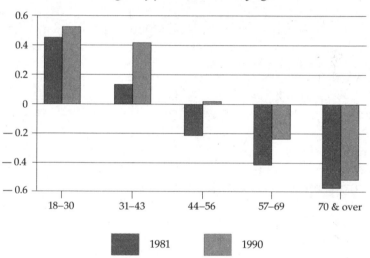

The survey[1] found, to no one's great surprise, that younger people tended to be more permissive than older people; Figure 5.1 shows they had positive scores whereas older people had negative. The key comparison, however, in Figure 5.1 is between the score in one age group in 1981 and the score in the *next* age group in 1990. Thus, for example, those aged 18 to 30 scored +0.45 in 1981 and +0.42 in 1990 when most would have been in the age range 31 to 43 – no change. Those aged 31 to 43 in 1981 had a score of

+0.14 and those aged 44 to 56 a score +0.04 in 1990, again virtually no change. The same is true for those aged 44 to 56 in 1981 and those aged 57 to 69 in 1990, and those aged 57 to 69 in 1981 and those 70 or over in 1990.

In other words, the permissiveness that a person had in his/her early 20s had not changed nine years later, nor had the permissiveness of a person in his/her early 30s, although this was lower than for those in their 20s. It may be concluded that permissiveness does not change with age, although it does change over time with successive cohorts.

This is an important finding. Once fixed, the 'value' of permissiveness did not change. True, it was only measured over one nine-year period, so it will be fascinating to see whether the results from 1999 confirm the trend. Also, it was only measured on permissiveness. How far is that value typical of all values? And is it a value, or an attitude? These are almost impossible questions to answer. This one finding, if true of values generally, suggests that our values, once formed in our 20s, do not then subsequently change significantly. In that sense, our values are forever.

However, our attitudes, our 'disposition' as the Oxford English Dictionary (OED) defines them, our 'settled mode of thinking', undoubtedly do change. Over the last three decades of the 20th century there have been great changes in people's attitudes to abortion, homosexuality and living together, for example. The British Social Attitudes surveys regularly measure such changes. Figure 5.2 illustrates their findings on attitudes towards homosexuality.[2] It is clear that younger people are more open than older, but, importantly, that both groups became more open in the 15 years 1985 to 2000. Their attitudes had certainly changed.

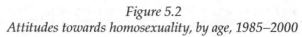

Figure 5.2
Attitudes towards homosexuality, by age, 1985–2000

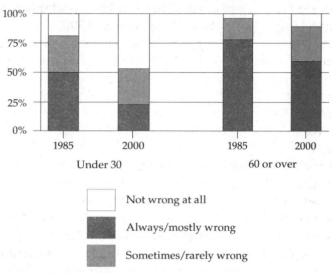

In this context our values are taken as defined by the OED as 'our principles or standards, our judgement of what is valuable or important in life, those which we prize, esteem or appreciate'. The dictionary gives as an example 'to value sincerity beyond all things'.[3] This would seem to suggest that our values are deeper than our attitudes, and in some way mould them. It would also suggest that, given sufficient exposure to other ideas, if our attitudes can change, then presumably our values to some extent can also.

This brief excursus into our value systems does not invalidate HMM, however. We ask people to express their values at one moment in time, and then apply those values to a future objective. By the time that objective is reached, say, ten years later, their values and/or their attitudes may have changed, but that does not mean the formation of those objectives at the beginning was wrong or incorrect or improper in some way.

Horizon Mission Methodology

At a meeting of the National Aeronautics and Space Administration (NASA) in 1994 someone is said to have asked, 'What will the world be like in 2100?'

Someone replied, 'People will be living on Mars then.'

'I'm not sure about that,' responded someone else.

A new voice entered the discussion. 'Let's not worry for the moment whether it is true. Let us assume that people will be living on Mars in 2100. What do we have to do between 2000 and 2010 to ensure that it comes true?'

And that is the vital breakthrough question!

In terms of most businesses, agencies and churches the NASA timescale of 2100 is far too long. Unless we are Shell looking for oil deposits, most of our timescales are set at five or ten years, 20 years at the most. The Tomorrow Project is one of the few organisations deliberately seeking to look 20 years ahead. Its first publication[4] in May 2000, subtitled 'Using the Future to Understand the Present', gave various scenarios over the years 2000 to 2020.

The essence of NASA's question, however, is still relevant. It is quite possible to rephrase it, 'If your church or organisation is to become like X [the equivalent of a person on Mars] in ten years' time, what does it have to do in the next year?' ('ten years' and 'year' can be any convenient periods of time).

The discussion at NASA was clearly stimulating. Subsequently a paper was written for *Futures Research Quarterly*,[5] which propounded Horizon Missions Methodology, and this technique has since gone under that name, usually abbreviated for convenience to just HMM.

The essence of the technique is:

- To imagine the future as a doorway, part of which can be seen by looking through a peephole in the doorway of the present.
- To imagine you are at the future doorway, and looking through a peephole in that door *back* towards the present doorway.
- To imagine that what you then see in the present doorway is in fact an expanded field of present knowledge.

This may be illustrated as follows, taken from the *Futures Research Quarterly* article:

Figure 5.3
Graphic depiction of HMM

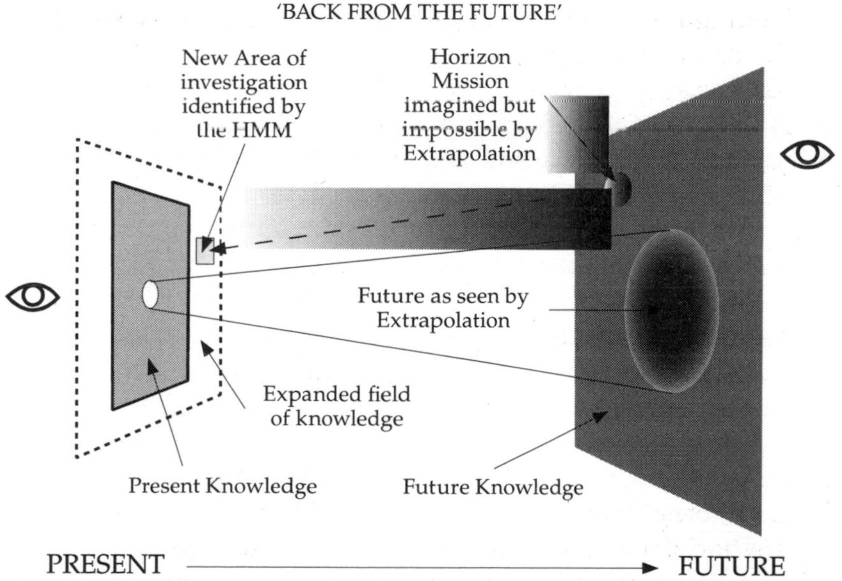

'BACK FROM THE FUTURE'

New Area of investigation identified by the HMM

Horizon Mission imagined but impossible by Extrapolation

Future as seen by Extrapolation

Expanded field of knowledge

Present Knowledge

Future Knowledge

PRESENT ──────────────────→ FUTURE

These 'imaginations' provide another means of strategic thinking. In effect it is to look at the future, not by extrapolating from the past and present (as Vision Building did), but by coming back to the near future from the viewpoint of the distant future. It is an interesting process, which seems to work! It makes the key assumption, however, that *the values driving people in a church or society transposed into the future will be the same as the values those identical people have in the church or society today.* This is a reasonable assumption, since it is the same people involved in both timeframes. We are not asking what will be the values in society in, say, 50 years' time, but what are the values of present-day people if they were time-travelled to 50 years hence.

Making it work

HMM can be applied to the church scene just as it can to any secular organisation. It does not seem to have been used greatly in a Christian context, although one attempt was made in an African situation. Perhaps it has been, and is being, used but simply not published. A shorter version of the paragraphs below was given in an earlier book.[6]

The essence of HMM is to travel, as it were, into the future and, as the author Wolfgang Grulke[7] points out, to learn from the future. To help people do that, Christian Research in its HMM Vision Building seminars presents a number of scenarios. Initially we had three such scenarios in a day, but have found that two work better. The purpose is to help the church or agency to think future, to imagine a vision of what it would like to become. It is not about describing the future, or even attempting to predict it in any serious way.

It is hard for people to think in radically different ways when they have been used to a given situation for perhaps many years. They know others in the organisation or congregation are familiar with their stories and the way they do things. To try and get them to consider new alternatives is not easy. So HMM suggests that they move to a situation that is new for everybody. In this way they all have a level playing field. The professor's experience may count for no more than the education of someone just out of school. Each has to imagine a different world. Some people's imaginations are better than others, but it does not follow that creative people will necessarily do best.

So what happens in these seminars? After a description of the process, a future scenario is described – examples to be given shortly. Those present are divided into groups of six to eight people and asked to react to what they have heard. We find it best if the groups are asked two questions at intervals, the first being a neutral, non-Christian question (to get them used to the idea of being many years hence!), and the second a specifically Christian question. Their answers are not written down, although to make the activity more lively the groups are sometimes asked to vote on which one they thought gave the best answers. Each person in the winning group then gets a packet of Polos, or something similar!

Subsequently they are asked *why* they gave the answers that they did, and these answers are written down so that everyone can see them (for example, on a flip chart or overhead projector slide). It is these answers which at least begin to tease out the values that were being applied in the future scene. This is where the assumption on values comes in, because *these future values are almost certainly the same ones* as drive them today.

When three scenarios were used, the second scenario would follow in the same way, and would be used to see if any new values emerged as a consequence. We found that very few new values emerged, even though the scenario might be quite different, and hence have concluded that one scenario instead of these two is usually sufficient. With only one scenario, you can spend longer in that time period, which enables people to think more deeply and enter into it more realistically.

Once the values have been listed and everyone has had the opportunity to contribute and indicate any that have been missed, they are asked to prioritise them. Each person chooses the three they feel most important and the three they feel important but not most important. We then go through the values one by one, asking those who felt them most important to put two hands up and those who felt them partly important just one hand. Counting the votes in this way determines the values the present audience feels are most important. It is worthwhile then helping people to reflect on the new list and to acknowledge that these are indeed the key values of the church or organisation. There is an additional question that is usually worth asking at this juncture: 'What values will you *not* sacrifice in order to accomplish your vision?'

The second scenario is usually one much closer to the present period of time, say ten or 15 years ahead. Its purpose is different. The aim now is not to determine the values but to try and uncover the implicit assumptions people are making on the changes they expect to have taken place over these next few years in their situation. These again are listed on a flip chart or overhead projector, and are again prioritised. We then have two lists – values deemed most important, changes most expected to have been made. Sometimes there is overlap between the two.

By this time people are usually 'hooked' and there is often an excited buzz of conversation over the lunch break.

When we get back together we start to apply the two lists created in the morning, starting with the top issues which emerged from the changes. Groups are asked each to come back with up to three practical actions that they feel should begin to happen immediately in the church or agency. There can well be overlap in their answers, which are again noted down.

Some of these suggestions are readily and easily applied, but sometimes a BHAG emerges. This is why this process is creative. I always tell the organiser, if asked to lead a Vision Building seminar in this way, that I cannot guess what the outcome will be in advance.

BHAG? This stands for **B**ig **H**airy **A**udacious **G**oal, and is usually said 'Be-hag'! It is an American term. It is:

> a powerful mechanism in an organisation. More than a goal, a BHAG is a 'take the mountain' kind of challenge. A BHAG is clear and compelling and serves as a unifying focal point of effort. It also requires a high level of commitment, not to the leader, but to the goal. It is not a statement but must engage and capture people's spirit.[8]

When President John F. Kennedy announced in 1961 that he wanted to see a man on the moon by the end of the 1960s, that was a BHAG. It thrilled and excited many people across America.

> A BHAG engages people – it reaches out and grabs them in the gut. It is tangible, energising, highly focused. People 'get it' right away; it takes little or no explanation.[9]

This is the process. Having led dozens of Vision Building seminars for churches and agencies using the Vision Building method described in the last chapter, what I find interesting is that given the choice everyone now chooses HMM as their preferred method for the day!

Examples of long-range future scenarios

To help you understand the process, let me give some of the scenarios that we have used. No attempt is made to make them scientifically sensible or reasonable, and if people want more information I always tell them to make it up!

Meteorite hits Isle of Man

It is the year 2050. In 2045 scientists discovered that a meteorite was going to hit the earth in 2050. Place of hit: Isle of Man. When it hit, it devastated Northern Ireland, the west coast of Scotland, most of north Wales and north-west England.

There was a massive earthquake and tidal wave. The top of Snowdon remained above the water, however. Huge waves were sent around Scotland and down the North Sea towards the English Channel. East Anglia was devastated. The flood barriers weren't high enough to protect London and much of the south-east is therefore as badly flooded as the Belfast and Glasgow regions. The Tower of London, Buckingham Palace and St Paul's are all under water. The tops of Canary Wharf and its nearby companion towers are just above it. The tidal wave created a new coastline for Britain.

All buildings over 30 feet tall have received severe structural damage. Virtually all churches are therefore unsafe to use. Many of those living in flats are homeless. Those in two-storey blocks are largely unscathed, however. Insurance damage money is already paid and in the bank (due to high electronic surveillance verification methods).

Thousands drowned; millions are homeless. The flood waters stopped a mile from your church, but everything around is damaged. It is now one month post-meteorite hit. You are a member of your Church Council.

- What are the greatest needs of your community and how are they being met?

- As a Church Council, what are your priorities for the next six months?

Future families no longer blood related

Over the first three decades of the 21st century, the Government gradually introduced more and more discriminations against marriage. Family Credits were discontinued and similar financial helps of every kind were stopped. Lone parents, same-sex couples and single people increasingly were allowed to adopt children, and adoption laws were slackened so that children could spend a few years with this person or couple and then the next few years with another. Eventually even the word 'family' was dropped. People simply lived in groups of adults and children that were recognised purely on the basis of 'loving and caring for each other'.[10]

'Mother' and 'father' became disused words, with children encouraged to call the adults in their current household by their first names. Blood relationships, while accepted where necessary, were increasingly becoming something that carried no definition of a meaningful or responsibility-carrying relationship.

In any case, because eggs and sperm could be manipulated at will in many laboratories, with designer babies and human cloning readily available, the significance of traditional 20th-century methods of procreation had diminished.

By 2040, sexually transmitted diseases had rapidly increased, and outstripped medical ability to curb or cure them. Some 60% of the adult population suffered from at least one such disease. Prostitution was no longer a criminal activity. Casual sexual activity was the norm, starting usually in junior school, where an eight-year-old recently gave birth to her first child.

Lack of funds from a supporting Diocese had led Agency X, working with parents and children, to expand its work from just that Diocese to nationwide in the 2020s, but numbers going to church decreased so much in the following years that the Diocese went bankrupt in 2030. Agency X struggled on for a few more years, but went bankrupt itself in 2040. However, concern for helping homeless children, giving advice to adults and trying to encourage some to undertake legal adoptions continued.

You are a member of the Leadership Team meeting to decide whether a new organisation like Agency X should be launched.

- What are the greatest needs of your community and how could they be met?
- As a Leadership Team, what are your priorities for the next five years?

Crash at Heathrow

In 2050 'jumbo' jets carry 3,000 people, not 300. Their wingspan is twice as big, but more powerful engines allow use of existing runways, so Heathrow is still in use. These jets have an excellent accident-free record.

Parents can now buy rocket-building kits for their children, which can ascend up to 5,000 feet. One boy lets one off illegally as a jumbo jet passes overhead and brings it down. It crashes near Heathrow.

A major fire destroys 90% of the nearby area, including your church. The fire brigade was unable to cope. Two of your Elders were also killed. Internet claim mechanisms have allowed insurance to be paid already.

- What are some of the main feelings in your community at this time?

- You are one of the remaining Elders, meeting two months after the crash to discuss rebuilding the church. What features do you wish to see in your new building? Please draw what it would look like.

Everyone going blind

Global warming reached danger levels in the 2030s, with excessive carbon dioxide in the atmosphere. Consequently, all vegetation that had previously grown green by 2030 was growing bright red – bright red grass, bright red trees, bushes, etc. However, the eyes of human beings were not able to adapt to so much bright red, and so everyone was going blind by the time they were 30, unless brought up in areas where there was no natural vegetation. So Inuit (Eskimos) and Saharan nomads are now the world leaders. A few people in Scotland are able to see.

- How are people preparing for their inevitable blindness? Is there general panic? What actions is the Government taking to help people?
- All Christian denominations now have Global Church Councils. You are some of the leaders of the European Branch of your Global Church Council, meeting to discuss evangelism for the next decade. What actions will you be proposing?

NATO bombed

The year is 2050. NATO has grown to 35 countries in the Northern Hemisphere, and has become much more pro-active in controlling world peace. Hence there is increasing resentment to it in some quarters. Active resistance is growing. The NATO base in Northwood is a target for many demonstrations to that effect. In 2050 a large bomb went off very near to it, bombs being much more powerful by then.

As a consequence, 75% of Harrow has been flattened, including Church X, a large Anglican church. Many church members have died, including all the clergy and other full-time staff. 75% of PCC members, living further away, have survived.

- How have people in Northwood reacted to this catastrophe? Is there a general desire to move out of the area or are people willing to stick it out if changes are made? What has been the response of the local Borough authorities?

- You are one of those who survived, and are meeting one month after the bomb went off to discuss the work of the church for the next twelve months. What are the top three actions that you will be taking?

Examples of shorter-range future scenarios

The above are examples of long-range scenarios, designed to try and help formulate the values of those in the church or organisation. We then use a second, more local, scenario, not so far ahead. Examples of these are:

Denominations forced to merge

The year is 2020. The British Government has become increasingly tired of the church's failure to be active in the social fabric of the country, and has passed a law forcing all churches in a locality to unite into a single unit, with one governing body looking after a maximum of two church buildings. The space for the rest is wanted for more housing. All denominations are therefore forced to work together.

Churches Together in Location X is now the governing body. Each of the churches brought into this body is allowed two representatives on the Council.

- You are meeting to advise your two representatives what line to take. What are the key programmes that your Church Council wants its representatives to stand for?

Church of England disestablished

The year is 2020. The Church of England has been disestablished. St X's now functions as an independent church. The Church Council is responsible for supporting all the staff, programmes and work of the church, and is responsible for hiring and firing all staff.

All costs have risen exactly fivefold. The church budget is now £1 million. You don't have to pay for maintenance on the church itself, however. As part of the disestablishment settlement English Heritage is able legally to enforce a 20% tax each year on the church, but it pays all maintenance and running costs. It has the power to close the church, though, if it doesn't pay for itself over a five-year period. So you have £800,000 to spend. The ministry costs of salary and housing are £150,000 [it is 2020!], and all the other staff cost £100,000 per annum, with part-time staff paid pro rata.

- You are on the Church Finance Committee working out next year's budget. What are the key items of expenditure? Each staff member is to be identified in functional terms (e.g. vicar to give vision and leadership to the church, etc.).

Episcopal visitation

The year is 2015, and you have a new Diocesan Bishop. He has decided this year to have episcopal visitations rather than those from Archdeacons, so will be personally visiting your PCC. He has already indicated that he would like answers to two questions that he wishes to discuss with you. These are the questions, and you are part of the group beginning to formulate the answers, which you will be asked to present:

- What has been your most successful outreach venture over the past five years?
- What will be your principal activity over the next five years?

This can be quite difficult, as people are being asked from a future perspective to look backwards as well as forwards! It is appreciated this example is entirely Anglican, but the terminology can be changed to accommodate other denominations.

Does it work?

The purpose of HMM is to help a church gain a vision and to think strategically as to how that vision may be accomplished. It is based on values and creativity. Sometimes what emerges is a plethora of what might be described as mini-visions. When that happened in one church, the minister was delighted – 'You've given me my programme for the coming year or so!' On the other hand, sometimes a BHAG emerges – one church decided to build a new church hall in order realistically to meet the needs of those on the estate.

The values that emerge are often one of three broad types, and frequently emerge in this order:

1) The need to *share* the information or resources which those in the church had with those without access to such.

2) The need to *help* people in their social, physical or family circumstances. This is essentially the desire to work in, with and for the local community.

3) The desire to *provide* opportunities for people to hear the Gospel or learn about what the church believes.

What is different with HMM?

Horizon Mission Methodology does not work in the same way as the Vision Building method. Table 5.4 shows some of the differences.

Table 5.4
Different ways of vision formation

Vision Building	Horizon Mission Methodology
Developed by management consultants	Developed by NASA scientists
Moves from past to near future	Moves from distant future to near future
Invariably linear	Rarely linear
Logical, progressive	Intuitive, creative
Focuses on statements	Focuses on values
Strategic planning a part of the process	Strategic planning a separate process
Few BHAGs	More BHAGs

Some years ago, the Chair of one of the larger evangelical mission agencies asked Christian Research to help with a Vision Building day. At that time we did not know of HMM so used the traditional method. A year or so later, a church in Southampton asked us to run a Vision Building day for them, and in discussion with the pastor, we used HMM. Imagine my surprise when the Chair of the agency turned out to be one of the deacons of the church!

As he personally experienced both methods I asked him for his reactions. The traditional Vision Building seminar, he said, helps to sharpen thinking and praying. It can be used to challenge others as it focuses on specific goals.

It allowed extrapolation and he felt it challenged leaders to return to core values. Horizon Mission Methodology, on the other hand, threw up many interesting concepts and possibilities. He felt it allowed ideas from more people to be heard, and thus encouraged a more inclusive ministry. He thought thinking future would inspire some to dynamic involvement, but proposed that it was easier for churches to change direction than agencies, and that therefore HMM was perhaps more useful for churches.

This was a helpful comparison. It shows the specific nature of Vision Building which is readily appreciated, but also shows that as HMM is wide ranging across both ideas and people, it offers greater opportunities for involvement.

Looking in a different direction

Trying to look to the future by looking backwards may seem an odd phenomenon. I enjoy taking holidays in Scotland, where the majestic beauty is often awesome. Going along some of the minor roads, you come across isolated houses or cottages facing magnificent scenery. Sometimes, however, you find such houses facing tangentially to the major view, as if they were built facing the wrong direction! There may be good reasons for this, like the prevailing winds, but it means that the owners don't naturally look at the view ahead when in their front room.

Perhaps the wild and beautiful scenery is already so much in their souls that they don't need to look repeatedly at it. The vision is so imbedded within them that they can look elsewhere (in other directions) for all the subsidiary things that are part of everyday life. HMM can be big enough to give such a sure vision that you can look at other facets of the process with confidence.

'When God gives you a vision, He doesn't usually give you a map, but He does give you a compass-bearing.'[11]

Diamonds!

This is Horizon Mission Methodology, a values-based method to enable vision formation with the challenge of subsequently needing to think strategically as to how it might be worked out. The vision and the thinking towards it are separated in HMM; in Vision Building they come as part of the package, as it were. While that makes for a shorter chapter, it also means greater subsequent discipline to work it carefully through. It also carries a challenge for the values one espouses: what will you *not* sacrifice in order to get there?

Notes

[1] David Barker, Loek Halman and Astrid Vloet, *The European Values Study*, Summary Report, Gordon Cook Foundation on behalf of the European Values Group, The Netherlands, December 1992, p. 32, second diagram.

[2] Alison Park et al (eds), *British Social Attitudes: The 19th Report* (London: SAGE and the National Centre for Social Research, 2002, pp. 218–20.

[3] J.B. Sykes (ed.), *Oxford English Dictionary* (Oxford: Oxford University Press, 1964) but reprinted many times subsequently.

[4] Richard Worsley and Revd Dr Michael Moynagh, *Tomorrow* (London: LexiCon Editorial Services, May 2000).

[5] John L. Anderson, 'The Horizon Mission Methodology: Modelling and Thinking within New Paradigms', *Futures Research Quarterly*, Fall 1995.

[6] Peter Brierley, *Steps to the Future* (Scripture Union, Bletchley, Milton Keynes and Christian Research, London, 2000), pp. 84, 85.

[7] Wolfgang Grulke and Gus Silber, *Ten Lessons from the Future* (@One Communications, Parklands, South Africa, 2000), p. 143.

[8] Article 'The Importance of a BHAG', *Next*, May 1997, p. 2.

[9] Ibid.

[10] In an extensive survey of 2,200 young people in 2002, 57% identified a family as meaning those who 'loved and cared for each other'. See *Reaching and Keeping Tweenagers*, Dr Peter Brierley, Christian Research, London, 2003.

[11] Christian speaker Marc Dupont, June 2002.

Chapter 6

♥ Relating and Delegating

Hearts are, of course, to do with people, and people involve relationships. People tell stories, share together, talk together. This method of strategic thinking is totally different from the other three, and if this method is not you, don't worry! But for those for whom it is, it can be of immense significance. Perhaps this method is best conveyed by illustration. As the key characters are so important, I've named them; they are real; all other names are imaginary. It was simply one of the most amazing meetings of my life!

The opportunities

Cape Town, South Africa

Having gone all the way to Kenya to visit our orphanage for 60 children, I took the opportunity to visit my cousin, who lives in South Africa, whom I hadn't seen for some years. I had never visited Cape Town, so I decided to spend a few days there also. Little did I know what was in store for me! A close friend told me I must meet Willie Crew while in Johannesburg, as he had such a vision for mission. He has! But he also knew many people, and in a busy hour before he left on a journey, he arranged for me to meet John Thomas in Cape Town.

Radio ministry

John came to the Fish Hoek[1] suburb of Cape Town in 1987 as the minister of the 30-strong Baptist church. Six years later, in 1993, the church had grown to 200 people. He was thinking about how best he could evangelise his neighbourhood and wondered if he could use the local radio network. He phoned the Government to ask if it might be possible, as an experiment, for him to broadcast for an hour or two every day for a week just to the people of Fish Hoek. Such requests had to be put in writing, the authority replied, so John duly did that.

The answer that came back surprised him. No, he could not broadcast for a couple of hours a day, but he would be allowed to do so for 24 hours a day. No, he couldn't do it for a week – it had to be for a month. No, he couldn't do it for the Fish Hoek area, but a much wider area around Cape Town. And, said the authority's letter, your licence begins in three weeks' time. This was the first licence the Government had ever granted to any group outside of Government-controlled stations. John had no money, no equipment, no programmes, no people – and very little time! A huge strategic challenge: what would you have done?

The next day John called on one of his church members at work and explained the opportunity that had been given.

'What do you want me to do about it?' asked Bill, thrilled at the opening presented.

'I want you to take a month's unpaid leave', said John, 'to help me make it happen.'

'When do you want me to start?' Bill replied.

'Tomorrow,' said John.

Bill did! In those three weeks the entire church got involved and found the money, bought the equipment, installed a transmitter, found people who could produce programmes, and made it happen. Phew! That was a busy time, but in the month that followed they received 13,000 letters from listeners begging them to continue. 'OK by us,' said the radio authority. So, with a deep breath, they took the plunge and continued. They didn't know then that 13% of the population of Western Cape (in which Cape Town is situated), the highest proportion in South Africa, were community radio listeners. Seven years later they were the biggest community radio station in the whole of South Africa!

Organising the radio ministry

The church hall of the Baptist church was small, about 500 square feet. Into that space they packed spare equipment, people to organise programmes and the studio for the live broadcasts. All was run by a small and dedicated team of volunteers – not paid staff. As the work expanded, space was at a premium, and it became obvious they would have to move elsewhere.

John looked at many houses but nothing seemed right. On one visit he was told that the house he had called at was not for sale, but rather the building next door. It was the place General Smuts had used when visiting Cape Town as Prime Minister after the Second World War. John liked the building, thought it would be suitable, and asked the price. I've forgotten the figure he gave me in South African Rand, but say it was £70,000. A third had to be put down as a deposit within a fortnight and the remainder paid a further month after that. He had little money.

Later that day, someone he knew came to lunch and gave him an envelope – 'for the radio building', she said. When John opened it he found a cheque for £10,000. A few days later someone he hardly knew gave another £10,000! John took this as God's seal that he was to purchase this building for the radio ministry. Nothing further was given in the next three weeks, but what he already had proved sufficient as a deposit. Then he had an international phone call from someone who had heard of his ministry in Fish Hoek.

'Is there any way I can help you?' he was asked, so John explained about the building he was hoping to buy.

'How much do you need, and when do you need it?' John answered these questions and gave the details of his bank account.

'It will be there by 1st February,' the caller promised, and rang off. This was the date by which the final instalment had to be paid.

In the meantime, the legal agreements had to be drawn up, and naturally John talked with the solicitor negotiating the sale.

'Do you have the rest of the money, Mr Thomas, to complete the purchase?'

'No, not yet,' he replied, 'but it will come.'

'Could I ask where you expect the money to come from?' he was asked.

'A friend in America,' said John.

'You have his name and address?'

'Well, actually, no, I don't.'

'Do you have his phone number then? We need to make sure the transaction can go through.' The solicitor wanted to check all was well.

'No, I don't even have his phone number. He has got my bank details, though.'

'You are very trusting, Mr Thomas. What contingency plan do you have if your friend is unable to supply the necessary funds?'

'There is no contingency plan,' replied John.

No money came that week, the next week or the week after. The last week arrived, and by 5.00 p.m. on 31st January, with no money from America, John was getting worried. Did God really want them to have this building? The balance of the purchase price had to be paid at 9.00 a.m. the following morning, and although some extra funds had come in, he had nothing like enough to buy the house. He rang the bank to ask if any money had come into his account, and was told a firm 'No'.

At 8.20 a.m. the following morning, however, the bank rang him. 'We thought you'd like to know, Mr Thomas,' the caller said, 'someone's put a hell of a lot of money into your account!' (direct quote).

Radio headquarters

John took me round this three-storey building. It was truly ideal for what they were wanting and had sufficient space for expansion. It also had a beautiful view of the seashore! As we went along, we passed James.

'Hello, James, this is Peter,' said John. 'James, how is your mother? Last time we spoke she was ill. Is she getting better? We prayed for her, as you know.'

Then we met Joan. 'Joan, this is Peter,' said John. 'How's your family? Your youngest was having trouble at school, wasn't he? Has that been sorted now?'

Emily passed, a young Indian girl of about 11. 'That's Emily,' John explained. 'She's in charge of the children's programme.'

'In *charge*!' I replied. 'Goodness, what if she makes a mistake?'

'Oh, someone else can easily correct it in the following half hour slot,' replied John, 'but actually, she's very good, a natural for it.'

I'm not sure how long it took us to get to the top of the building, but a long time. John knew the name of every person we met and asked a question about his/her circumstances, health, family, job. He knew something about everyone. Here was someone who broke the normal rule that you can only know 150 people or so by name, and it was amazing to watch him in action.

'All volunteers,' he explained. 'We don't pay anyone any salary at all; we have 216 volunteers altogether at the moment.'

'216!' I replied, imagining the task of running an organisation with so many people. 'Who keeps track of them all?' It was a silly question.

'Oh, another volunteer!' he replied, which was doubtless true enough, but that volunteer was also greatly helped by his hard-working wife, Avril. They needed so many volunteers. They were broadcasting 24 hours a day, 7 days a week, all live broadcasts. Nothing was pre-recorded, except some of John's sermons. Services at the church were transmitted live on Sundays. In the year 2000, 600,000 people listened to religious radio in the six largest of South Africa's nine provinces, covering 83% of the population. One-third of these listened to John's station, Radio CCFm.[2]

Nelson Mandela, when President of South Africa, found it difficult to attend church on Sundays because of the attention he always drew. However, he often visited the President's weekend retreat house in Cape Town, and was a frequent listener to Radio CCFm. John Thomas found that out when he got to meet the President one day.

Radio expansion

During the period 1995 to 2002 the Baptist church doubled in size to 450 Sunday worshippers. The old building was replaced with a much larger church, based at an important intersection on a key highway. The new building, looking to my mind more like an enormous warehouse than a church, was called the King of Kings Baptist Church and could seat up to 1,500 people. In one of the rooms a series of A3 sheets decorated by children was placed around the wall.

Each sheet had the name of an African country written on it in large capital letters, but otherwise they were individually designed. 'Community radio has worked so well for us in South Africa', John explained, 'that we thought we would build similar facilities in every African country south of the Sahara.' The precise details I cannot now recall, but the conversation went something as follows.

'This is Angola. Joe's looking after this. We are uncertain as to the best location for the radio station due to the civil war, but we are working with the local church to think that through.

'This is Namibia. Tom, who works in our local police, has already raised the funds. They've worked out the best place and the station is in the process of being built, and should open in a few months' time. Some of the folk are coming for training in a week or so.

'This is Burundi. We decided that it would be good not just to build a radio station but a Bible College as well. However, the local people really need a hospital, so we're going to build that also. Francis has worked out that we can finance this through selling electricity to the Government, once we've built the dam.'

'How much will the dam cost?' I asked, and, in UK money, John went on ...

'Oh, about £10 million. Now, here's Zambia. Wesley, who makes furniture, is running with this one. He ...'

'Just a minute,' I interrupted. 'Did you say that your church is raising money to build a dam?'

'Yes,' he replied, 'that's right. In Zambia, we are finding that ... '

'But there's not another Baptist church in the world trying to build a dam,' I said, 'and it's not as if it's your only project.'

'No,' said John, 'we have others. Zambia is interesting because ...'

I'm afraid I was very rude and interrupted yet again. 'But £10 million is a huge amount of money,' I said. 'Where will you get it all from?'

'Oh, Francis has approached a number of trusts in America. I am sure the money will come in if God is behind it. In Zambia the situation is ... '

John was finally able to tell me about Zambia ... and Kenya ... and Tanzania ... and so it went on. Here was a pastor with the whole of Africa south of the Sahara in his vision. Amazing!

The AIDS project

John kindly said he would drive me to my next appointment. On the way we passed an African shanty town. Had I ever been in one? Yes, some years ago I visited one in Alexandria and twice went to Soweto.

'Never mind,' said John, 'I'll take you round this one,' and we drove in. 'See that couple over there?' he asked. 'One of them has AIDS. See those two boys playing football? One of them will be HIV positive.' The percentage of people in shanty towns with AIDS was 40%.

'We built this church for them', John continued as we passed a tall, imposing building, 'and have reached an agreement with the local authorities that only those who have been through the church's counselling courses can register for AIDS help. We've had to work out a whole new way of talking to people about sin.'

He took me through the shanty town, and I expressed my gratitude, but he wasn't finished.

'When I came back from holiday last year, I noticed that plot of land was for sale, the last plot available in this area. So I bought it straight away, that morning. On the following Sunday I asked the Church Council if they would like to buy it from me for development as an AIDS hospital. Had they said no, I could have sold it easily enough as plots for houses, but they agreed. Come and see it; it was an old pub. We're converting it into a counselling centre.'

We went to the pub, which was in an obvious state of refurbishment. 'Hi there, Fred,' he called out. 'Just me. Oh, this is Peter. How's your water system – is it working now?'

'Yes, thanks, John,' replied Fred. 'Mike came round as you suggested and sorted it. It's fine now, thank you very much.'

'Everything else OK?'

'Well, the guttering here is coming down. Look, I'll show you,' said Fred, and took John to see it.

'That's no problem,' said John, 'I'll ask Harry to call. He's good at fixing things like that.'

We came outside and John pointed to an empty corner of the field. 'See that area?' he asked. 'That's where we are going to build an AIDS hospital. Two storeys if we can. I've asked Jack if he can sort out the finance and he's already been to Charlie, our architect. Now we're waiting to get planning permission.'

Why tell all this?

I was with Revd John Thomas for about four hours that afternoon and by the time I left I was completely stunned. Never have so many projects, visions, people been presented to me so quickly and never with such detachment, humility and trust that God would work it all out. I had no doubt that the Lord had led him into a remarkable ministry, but he made me wonder what it was that excited me so much. For he had shown me a whole new way of working that I hadn't consciously met before. I also felt very clearly that he was taking strategic opportunities time and again in a way that few did.

Why is this important in a book primarily looking at strategic thinking? John Thomas was probably not a strategic thinker, but a strategic opportunist.

He could sense what was important to do and went ahead without hesitation to try and do it. I suppose he had what might be called 'strategic vision' or 'strategic visions', for visions seemed to trip off his tongue faster than you could absorb them!

John Thomas was probably not a leader according to the Belbin definition. He would not have fitted comfortably into either a Director or Shaper mode, but he was unquestionably in a position of leadership, and dispensed that leadership everywhere he went. He was far too entrepreneurial to ever work in the Civil Service! Time and again, he simply gave his leadership, his vision, away, totally away. Subsequently he would check up on how it was going, and take corrective action where necessary, but his role was supportive after passing on his vision, coming in only as asked to do so. If things were going wrong, however, I suspect he would step in quickly to sort them out.

John Thomas was unquestionably a people-person. Team-related to a T! He simply loved people, and wanted them to find Jesus if they didn't know Him, or serve Jesus if they did. His knowledge of names, situations and gifts was exceedingly impressive. But it wasn't just his knowledge; he was clearly open and honest. It would be easy to trust him, confide in him, knowing any secret was safe. He cared for you, and epitomised Jesus' command that we should love one another. It was obvious he acted with integrity, and people respected him for it. He wouldn't always get things right, but he would always be supported for trying to do something to help.

He made me realise that here is a way of operating that is as important as any carefully planned strategic operation, or any project that may emerge from a Vision Building day, or any BHAG that Horizon Mission Methodology might generate. In some ways, his method was far more powerful, for he was looking after not one project, but probably fifty. I don't suppose he ever bothered even to count them! In a book on strategic thinking, it seems to me that strategic opportunism and strategic vision very definitely have a place!

Relating and Delegating

The wording needs to be formalised. What, in essence, was the core of what John Thomas was doing? Perhaps it could be described like this:

> The ability to achieve multiple projects simultaneously through delegation of total vision fulfilment to those trusted people deemed highly likely to be capable of carrying them out on time.

There are a number of implications in this definition:

- It is the *vision* that is delegated, not the project *per se*. Of course the administrative work, finance raising and everything else comes with the vision, but it is not a project that is given away, but the vision. 'Giving the people of Namibia community radio' was the vision, not 'building a radio station in Windhoek [the capital of Namibia]'. He gave away the 'why' and did not direct the 'how'.

- It requires an *extensive knowledge of people* and their experience and gifts. This is relational leadership, leading, as a shepherd might, from thoroughly knowing a flock. Naturally those thus entrusted are conscious of the privilege that is theirs. Many are businesspeople. They are appointed owners of a vision, and asked to fulfil it. What a thrill!

- This requires an ability to see *multiple opportunities*. While the detail is important, and can be worked out as necessary, the reality is that most of the time is spent at helicopter level spying out the openings. Like Alexander Fleming, the discoverer of penicillin, as he was doing the dishes one day in September 1928, John Thomas had the eye to appreciate the opening (or notice the unusual) and the mind to grasp its significance. That has to be a type of strategic thinking! It means an ability to ponder the unusual, not despising the mundane, and realising that discontinuity with past methods or traditions is possible. 'Seeing what others don't' is how the Royal Bank of Canada describes this trait.[3]

- There is an ability to *translate the invisible* into the visible. Behind the various visions John generated, there was the desire to see more and more people come to Christ. This was his overwhelming desire, rarely articulated unless a direct question was asked, but nevertheless the driving grand strategic objective he was concerned to try and achieve. This invisible drive provided the key motivation behind the man. 'Love for people' is too weak a phrase to describe this; 'dominant passion' is perhaps closer.

- There is probably an *implied hierarchy* here. A person running with a vision is usually thought of as the leader of the project. But a person running with 50-plus visions is hardly a leader of 50-plus leaders – it's too many. Actually, it's not like being in a helicopter – you simply can't see far enough. You have to be in Concorde, cruising at 60,000 feet, with the clouds far below you, and the sky a beautiful ultramarine rather than a bright blue! As Concorde pilots were fairly scarce, even when it was regularly flying, that could suggest why the John Thomases of this world are fairly scarce also. Most of us are simply not far-sighted enough, too attached to present realities, and not quick enough to grasp a Kingdom opportunity.

- There is also *naked faith*, a God-given gift. Like Hudson Taylor, who in faith sent missionaries to China in the mid–19th century, those so delegating to others not only receive the Lord's visions, but trust unequivocally in God to supply the means and people to fulfil them.

There are others!

Special as John Thomas may be in Cape Town, there are others with the same kind of gifts even in the UK! Revd Brian Meardon is Vicar of Warfield, a parish near Bracknell in Berkshire, part of the more wealthy commuter belt. His congregation includes many businesspeople working in management in London. He became vicar in the early 1980s, and soon realised the potential in the parish.

Over time three new congregations came into existence, one with a particularly youthful flavour, in addition to the one he inherited, meeting in local schools. To cope with the leadership work, Brian appointed a single person who was primarily responsible for each congregation, and was fortunate in having capable people in his congregation who could handle this delegated responsibility. This arrangement worked very happily, so he appointed someone to run his own church too! He was giving away his vision.

Each leader was encouraged to gather around him (they were all men) others who would form an appropriate team for that congregation's leadership (which included a number of women).

All these were within the one parish. So there was only one PCC, only two church wardens. An oversight team was constructed of the four congregational leaders, church wardens, church treasurer and vicar, which reported to the PCC. This arrangement worked well, and total numbers attending these different congregations grew sevenfold in about twenty years.

The pressure of work on Brian grew likewise, and eventually reached dangerous levels of stress, so an Associate Vicar was appointed, together with a senior-level administration team. As a consequence, Brian was free to spot other openings in order to start further congregations. No longer grounded, his Concorde could fly again!

This example may be on a smaller scale than that described in Fish Hoek, but the factors at work are very similar. The 'Relating and Delegating' model described fits both. Having met both Brian and John, their personalities are very similar also. They both know what they want to do, and both yearn to get on and do it – through others. Like John, Brian has a keen sense of the invisible.

Other methods of strategic thinking can be taught. I don't think this one can be; a person either has this relational and delegating gift or he/she hasn't. If you haven't got it, don't try and manufacture it! You might perhaps catch such a gift from working closely with someone who has it, but I'm not sure.

There are, however, consequences on both the person who has the gift and on the teams that are created which have implications beyond this particular mode of working, so these are briefly discussed in the remaining pages of this chapter.

The stress

Stress comes in many ways, and it may be a particular hazard to those people able to work in the Relating and Delegating mode described. How can it be recognised? Another word for stress is 'pressure'; some pressure is self-generated.

Cary Cooper, who is Professor of Organisational Psychology at the University of Manchester Institute of Science and Technology (UMIST), has made a special study of managers, through the Institute of Management. These results are useful, because many church leaders operate with similar levels of responsibility to business managers, as the first chapter indicated, irrespective of whether they work in a Relating and Delegating manner.

He gives some practical observations:[4]

- *Time worked*: 80% of managers worked more than 40 hours a week, 40% worked more than 50 hours a week, 2% worked more than 80 hours a week. How many hours a week does the average minister work? This is not known generally, but a number of individual case studies put the average as between 50 and 55 hours a week. If universally true, ministers are already in a minority in terms of work practice!

- *Evenings worked*: 60% of managers were found often or always to work in the evenings. Many worked over the weekend as well. Clergy's jobs almost always require that they do both!

- *Pressure of time*: This is harder to measure, but 66% of managers said they felt under constant time pressure, with simply too much to do in too short a time. Many clergy would echo this finding also. In one large survey,[5] 78% of clergy said the amount of internal administration they were asked to do put pressure on them, and 60% the amount of external bureaucracy.

- *Home pressure*: The pressure in homes where both parents work, which is true of two families out of three, can be very intense. The Professor commented that 'The idea that parents can give quality time to their children or to each other when they are exhausted is a myth. Weekends filled with domestic chores increase the strain.'

- *Financial pressure*: The same survey[6] showed that 40% of clergy find it difficult to live on their stipend (rising to 59% for those aged 35 to 44). 53% of clergy augment their income through their spouse's paid employment. In addition, 58% of clergy reported the under-financing of their church as a key pressure point.

Alarm bells

What, then, are some of the warning signs or alarm bells that your personal pressure may be getting too great? Professor Cooper gives a long list, not suggesting that all have to be present, just some! These were:

> Losing your sense of humour
> Lack of concentration
> Difficulty making decisions
> Irritability
> Being more aggressive
> Insomnia
> Waking up tired
> Smoking more
> Loss of libido

Longing for a drink to buck you up

Overeating or undereating

Flatulence

Not taking care of appearance

Many years ago, when working in the Ministry of Defence, several of us had a boss whose memos from time to time became more aggressive and demanding. We all learned to recognise them, and said to each other in the office, 'It's time Barry went on holiday!'

There are characteristics of less strain also, but far fewer! These were:

Respect for home life

Element of 'fun' in the workplace

Handling pressure

If there is pressure, are you able to detect where it is coming from? Is it primarily through the church, other work, your home and family, your leisure pursuits, your particular circumstances, or other personal elements? Knowing the source doesn't stop the pressure, but at least recognising its source can help direct attention as to where it is coming from.

A second way of trying to identify pressure is to ask, 'What is it that you are not doing, or not having?' In other words, what effect is the pressure having on you? If you are waking up tired, for example, as I sometimes do, then part of the solution is simply to go to bed earlier, or get up later. It may well be that this requires discipline you don't feel you've got the energy to exert, but that isn't really a very good excuse!

Thirdly, a positive way of looking at the situation is to ask questions like: 'If money was no object, what would be your solution?' or 'If you could change one thing, what would it be?' This allows the opportunity to reflect on what you could do about the situation if you were able. It may not reduce the immediate pressure, but it opens up the possibility of taking action should the opportunity arise.

Different personalities handle pressure in different ways. A Relating and Delegating person will almost certainly look for a person who can carry some of the load. That's exactly what Brian Meardon did in seeking to appoint an Associate Vicar. The logical person who is comfortable with the Vision Building approach described in Chapter 4 may well sit down and work carefully through his/her current programme to see what can be stopped or deferred to ease the pressure. A more creative person may resolve stress best by doing something completely different for a few hours or days, coming back refreshed and invigorated.

In a detailed survey of charismatic ministers in 2000, Professor Leslie Francis found that when asked what their key training needs were, over half, 51%, the largest group, identified 'stress'. Two-fifths, 38%, said they were overwhelmed by pastoral care in their church, of which stress was the most frequent item (66%).[7]

Team leadership

A great deal has been written both about leadership in general and team leadership in particular, Christian and otherwise, and it is a topic to which we return in the last chapter. Here, therefore, we look at leadership within the context of working with a Relating and Delegating senior.

Team leader

Being the kind of person described above generates certain demands on the person when he/she is a team leader:

- There is the expectation of *success*. You have given the 'vision' to someone else, and while he/she will recognise the privilege of that, it carries also the weight of responsibility for carrying it out. His/her striving to do so could easily generate too great a stress for him/her, and that would then echo back to you. So you have to be content to allow his/her timing to be determinant in the fulfilment of the vision (which might well be different from yours!).

- For the person to whom the job has been delegated, there is also the expectation of success, or else presumably he/she wouldn't have taken on the job. But, if despite everything he/she (and you if asked) can think of, it doesn't work out, to some extent he/she can relax with the thought that he/she gave it his/her best shot. The job is about faithfulness in trying the action, not actually the reward of success. However, it is important that this doesn't become simply an excuse, as otherwise the overall leader might think it time for replacement therapy!

- There is the expectation usually that the work can be done *alongside* your existing responsibilities. Bill was asked to take a month's unpaid leave to exploit the original radio opportunity, and John was fortunate to have a person able to do this at short notice. Many simply cannot do that. Trying to do two things, your usual work during the day, and the extra work in the evenings or weekends, means that those asked to do this must be able to identify priorities very carefully.

- There is the freedom to *choose your own team*, and this freedom is also delegated downwards. This is where Brian had an advantage in being able to choose team leaders who were businesspeople (in the main) with experience of selecting staff and working in a team mode. Not everyone has that ability. Choosing people to work with you, however, especially if they are volunteers, is a large responsibility. Having a balanced team, *vis-à-vis* the Belbin description, is important.

To compensate, there are some big advantages in being able to work in this way:

- There is the freedom to work out *your own strategic plan*, though this is set within the limits of the grand strategy or vision. One of the features of this kind of leadership is that the detail is truly delegated to the person responsible. There is no one looking over your shoulder every minute, although you may look over other people's shoulders! They have the opportunity to come back to you and ask questions, or seek clarification, or to check out a proposed course of action, but you are equally able to ask others what they think, including members of any team you choose.

- You have the comfort of *knowing what the parameters* of the total vision are. You don't have to test the edges, or query its extent. You may wish to change its intensity ('if we did so-and-so, we could reach twice as many'), but you are not, to change the metaphor, about to rewire the house. You will not be producing suggestions like those labelled 'Y' in Figure 4.9!

Team member

Being a team member in one of these teams can be great fun! You have the opportunity to discuss at whatever depth you want to the project on which you are working. You have the opportunity to try your hand and gain valuable experience. You can see other people in action and learn from the way they do it. In terms of the terminology to be used in the next chapter, you are at the 'tactical' end of the work, where the rubber hits the road. As one person put it, you 'take your sunshine with you'.[8]

It can be exhausting also, and there can be the temptation to take on too much. But in the main, working in the team is an enjoyable experience, or at least it should be most of the time! You are helping to make the vision happen, and the success of that fulfilment will be sweet to every team member: 'It was worth it!'

There is also a strong sense of ownership of the vision. The biggest concern of the team leaders in Brian's church was that an Associate Vicar might impinge on their freedom and want to take back some of their responsibility.

Winning Teams

In his book,[9] Belbin has a chapter in which he describes what he calls 'winning teams'. They have the following characteristics:

- A chairperson or leader who is trusted to use the gifts and abilities of each team member correctly. No one is asked to do something outside his/her competence, unless specifically in a learning or training capacity to see how he/she gets on.

- Someone in the team who is creative, and can therefore help solve problems as they crop up, whether these be physical problems about the project, or personnel problems relating to team members, or communication problems. Belbin adds that it helps if such a person is clever as well!

- Across the team as a whole there is a spread of mental abilities. Belbin found that a team of PhDs invariably failed! Charles Handy, the management guru, describes eleven different intelligences[10] (given in the final chapter), and effectively Belbin is suggesting that a good range of these is needed.

- The team needs to consist of people who reflect seven of the eight roles that Belbin described (given in Chapter 1).

- The work team members are asked to do is in line not only with their gifting and experience but also with the contribution they bring to the team. If you have a critic, for example, make sure you run all your reports and public communications past him/her, as critics tend to spot items that everyone else misses!

- A shared consciousness of the weaknesses in the team. No team is perfect, and knowing what you haven't got as well as what you have can be a major strength. Why? Because the team then knows when it needs further external help, and doesn't try to keep soldiering on regardless.

Unsuccessful teams

The opposite of winning was not losing for Belbin, but rather being 'unsuccessful'.[11] Characteristics of such teams were:

- Poor team morale. This may seem an obvious factor, but Belbin comments that in reality it is only a marginal item; other things are much more important in whether a team wins through or not.

- An inadequate range of mental ability, which Belbin states is a critical factor. The combinations of intelligence, teams and leadership have not been explored very greatly, and rarely if at all in terms of Christian teams. The top 13 qualities of leadership, which the founder of the Haggai Institute for Advanced Leadership Training advocates in his book,[12] do not include intelligence!

- Personality clashes. Hence the pressure on the leader who has the responsibility of choosing the team. It means that 'exit' mechanisms need to be understood and in place from the start, but also that exercises are undertaken to ensure that the team learns to work together as much as it can.

- An unbalanced composition, as seen by the Belbin factors. If a team has too many of one kind, it is important that new members are drawn in who have other abilities.

- Nor does it help if team members are asked to act in ways that don't match their primary team contribution. Critics are best asked to act as critics, and not be expected to be creative people, except in an emergency! Square pegs in round holes are unacceptable for everyone.

- Every team member needs to have a specific responsibility. Belbin would be against the Cabinet concept of having a Minister without Portfolio. He felt every person should know what he/she was there for, and could make the appropriate contribution to the work.

- An inability of the team to think corporately, or, using other language, an inability to understand the vision. Those who see a job as purely a job without recognising how it fits into a wider whole are unhelpful members of a team. Teams have to think together, to understand the overall vision, and to appreciate the invisible that is being attempted, even if they had no direct part in its outworking.

Leadership and being team members are not quite as easy as they may sound!

Hearts!

Hearts are often depicted in T-shirt slogans, such as 'I ♥ NY', meaning 'I love New York'. They carry the implication of loving, of caring, of understanding. The successful person who relates and delegates can only do so if he/she really understand people. But knowing people is not the only key component.

They have to be able truly to give their vision away, together with the responsibility for its fulfilment. Too many want to delegate, but still have their finger in the pie. Even that isn't sufficient, however, for the rare breed of leaders described here. They also have to soar at high levels, bitten by their invisible goal, and to be able to translate that into many visions or sub-strategies. Thinking strategically without involving your heart will result in you becoming little more than an ideas machine.

Notes

[1] This *is* the correct way to spell this particular Fish Hoek; it follows the Dutch!

[2] Analysis based on a report, *Radio CCFm*, a radio audience measurement survey of 56 radio stations in six of South Africa's nine provinces (83% of the population) between November 1998 and December 2000.

[3] Royal Bank Letter, October 2001, p. 2.

[4] Taken from his 1997 survey of 1,390 Institute of Management managers.

[5] *The Mind of Anglicans*, undertaken for Cost of Conscience by Christian Research in 2002, with replies from 1,741 incumbents, 46% of those approached.

[6] Ibid.

[7] *Pastoral Care Today: An Interim Report of the Practice, Problems and Priorities in Churches Today*, commissioned by CWR/ Waverley Christian Counselling and the Evangelical Alliance, and undertaken by the Centre for Ministry Studies, University of Wales, Bangor by Professor Leslie Francis, Mandy Robbins and Revd Dr William Kay, published in September 2000. It was summarised in *Quadrant*, Bulletin of Christian Research, November 2000, p. 2.

[8] Jill Garrett speaking at the CEO Forum arranged jointly by the Evangelical Alliance and Christian Research on 26th September 2000.

9   R. Meredith Belbin, *Management Teams: Why they Succeed or Fail* (Butterworth-Heinemann, London, originally published in 1981 but very frequently reprinted), ch. 8.

10   Charles Handy, *The Hungry Spirit* (London: Hutchinson, 1997), but he omits a key twelfth intelligence – spiritual intelligence.

11   Belbin, *Management Teams*, ch. 7.

12   John Haggai, *Lead On!* (Waco, Texas: Word, 1986).

Chapter 7

♠ The Military Model

Spades are a fairly precise tool useful for digging. The dictionary goes further and adds that they have sharp edges and are used with both hands. Spades are, I am told, needed for removing the blubber from whales, a task that presumably requires a degree of accuracy. The phrase to 'call a spade a spade' means to speak plainly and bluntly. If you are 'in spades' when playing bridge it means you have a good, strong hand and can play with enhanced power.

Thus the word 'spades' seems a very reasonable one to describe our fourth mode of strategic thinking, which requires detail, accuracy, clarity and forcefulness. To describe it also as the 'Military Model' carries similar overtones.

In January 2002, Christian Research initiated an annual leadership lecture. The inaugural talk was given by Richard Dannatt, then a Major General, and was subsequently published in printed form.[1] We owe a huge debt of gratitude to him for the clarity, humility and helpfulness of his lecture. This chapter is based very largely upon it, and has simply expanded on what he said, using our experience in adapting it to help churches and agencies think forwards in Vision Building exercises. As so much of it emanated from such a source, the term 'Military Model' is doubly appropriate.

The Military Model must not, however, be considered as unyielding, irreversible and inflexible, like an invading army pushing all before it. Our television screens may reflect such an image of military prowess, but the reality of this method is one of detailed preparation and thorough thinking. It is readily adaptable to both the initial and changing circumstances to which this kind of thinking has to be applied.

The word 'military' carries with it an image of thoroughness, with nothing being left to chance and detail being thought through at all levels. It is a correct image for this type of thinking. The Vision Building method included within it the need for planning, the Horizon Mission Methodology method made strategic planning a separate exercise, and Relating and Delegating gave the task of planning to others. The Military Model of thinking includes planning at its core; in the terminology of Chapter 4 it is using the business and portcullis methods for relatively simple objectives, and scenario planning for the more complex (though the real military will almost certainly also use PERT [Programme Evaluation and Review Technique] for major operations).

Three levels of direction

This way of thinking future has three levels: strategic, operational and tactical. All require *thinking*, and while they are hierarchical, it should not be assumed that the type of thinking required at the top level is somehow superior to the type of thinking required at the lower level. It is simply a different type of thinking that is needed.

Strategic level

Thinking at this level means identifying items of strategic significance. This phrase means that:

to act strategically one must lay down realistic policy objectives and set out what it is you want or need to do. One must identify and set out what are the limitations within which one must work, and one must identify what resources could or should be made available.[2]

This definition has a number of implications.

set out what ... to do ...
Statements need to be made about objectives. Almost certainly these should be made in writing, which carries the further implication of wide availability or easy communication if necessary. Whatever the value of verbal memory (and in some cultures it has very high importance), for the large majority setting something out clearly requires writing it down.

what ... you ... need to do ...
The objectives should set out what needs to be done. These may be clearly known, even if very broad. The last command of Jesus to His disciples was 'Go therefore and make disciples of all nations' (Mt. 28:19), indicating very clearly what has to happen. This kind of statement is almost impersonal in its expression, although of course it will require people to fulfil it.

Archbishop William Temple's book *Towards the Conversion of England*, published in the 1940s, has a similar kind of detached imperative associated with it. It is a statement of intent, a purpose statement of the highest order.

what it is you want ...
The objectives, however, can also indicate personal vision. The scope for this is very much present at the strategic level. When one Baptist minister stated that he 'wanted to reach this town for Christ' in the 1960s he was articulating his

personal desire on the one hand, but stating something that he knew would require decades of work by a whole team of people on the other. It might have originated as a personal desire, but it quickly became an overarching objective for many who, while not themselves articulating such a statement, accepted willingly the implications of it.

realistic ... objectives ...
In Chapter 4 we saw that visions must be realistic. That is equally true of 'policy objectives', which in many ways is simply another phrase to describe 'visions'. Along with that realism comes clarity. Statements (or objectives or visions) that are too general are not activating or energising. Something that is specific can appeal to the imagination. 'Reaching this town for Christ' can be highly motivational.

limitations within which one must work ...
What is the geographical area within which these objectives operate? One of the benefits of the parish system used by the Anglican and Catholic churches is that the 'care of souls' given to incumbents or priests at their induction is a precise physical area now coming within their responsibility. They may have wider interests (such as sending people to help in Tanzania) but that derives from the base defined as their parish.

Limitations are not only geographical; financial ones abound. It may sound grand to have a strategy that costs £1 million, but if the church's annual income is only £50,000,[3] the strategy is unworkable, unless it includes some means for raising the money.

Personnel limitations also have to be identified. Is this objective so overriding that *everybody* in a church or agency is bent towards reaching it, or will some people continue other activities? For example, how much should the church be involved in evangelism as opposed to discipleship and the nurture of Christian people? The gifts, training and experience of the congregation or employees become relevant here.

resources ... made available ...
It may be easier to state your vision than to spell out what is required to make it happen! But the vision is unlikely to be fulfilled unless work is done to find out the cost, the number of people likely to be involved, the processes required and the time it is likely to take. A further step is to identify whether these resources are already available or will have to be found elsewhere. It is not just that resources have to be supplied, but it gives a comfort zone to those involved to know these things have been considered and that the vision is more than just a pious dream.

It is rather like the Chair in a meeting saying, 'I have my eye on the clock; we aim to finish by 10.00 p.m.' All present know that there is a terminus for the debate and that it is being actively worked towards. The current discussion may seem to be endless or going round in circles, but someone somewhere aims to be in control.

So it is with vision. Here is someone not only with a desire to see radical change, but who also knows how he/she would like to see it accomplished. It may turn out slightly differently as progress is made, but adapting plans already made is much more acceptable than making them up as one goes along!

Two levels of strategy

There are two levels to this kind of strategic thinking, however. Both are correctly described as 'strategic', but one encapsulates the other.

Grand strategic

These are top-level, overarching statements of hope and intent and purpose. The Great Commission of Jesus is one such strategic direction under which all subsequent church and agency activity is carried out. The designation of the 1990s as the 'Decade of Evangelism' was another such statement. These are the 'Concorde-level' ideas and directions, objectives that are wide and far ranging, from which lesser objectives may be deduced and applied.

Church or agency strategic

These are the more immediate 'realistic policy objectives' with given limitations and resources. It is in this level that most church leaders operate. Senior leaders, such as Bishops, will sometimes operate here and sometimes at the grand strategic level. Church and agency strategies tend to be those that are worked out in smaller churches, or with smaller, newer teams, or with people cautious of overextending themselves.

The differences between the grand strategic and the church/agency strategic follow very similar lines of thought to those expressed in the parameters of strategic thought discussed in Chapter 1.

Operational level

The second main tier of military strategy is the Operational Impact Level. This is where a leader converts his/her strategic objectives into practical activity. Strategy has to be worked out. In Chapter 4 the word 'Thrusts' was used for this step, though the concept is taken further here. These are the broad areas into which the strategy has to be divided. In military terminology, these are the different spheres of operations. There are three components to the thinking required here.

Deciding tactical objectives (goals)

In Table 4.1 these were termed 'Goals', the shorter-term aims that need to be met. Goals are specific measurable targets. They are, however, related to the strategic purpose by the question 'Why?' 'Why are you doing this?' is answered by reference back to the strategy. Asking of the strategy 'How will this be accomplished?' you point, in part, to the individual goals. How are the goals to be worked out? The portcullis method of planning described in Chapter 4 is relevant with such.

There is often confusion here in Christian gatherings. The word 'goal' comes from games such as football, where the objective is to get the ball into a net, following a given set of rules. If the person who kicks the ball falls over and doesn't see where it goes, the reaction of the crowd will soon tell him/her whether or not he/she scored.

In some Christian discussions, the concept of a goal is more akin to a field growing wheat and nearly ripe for harvest. In one seminar a church leader said that his goal was 'to evangelise his parish'. Such a picture might be summarised as 'a fruitful harvest', and much Christian activity could be identified as operating under that broad rubric. Working for a fruitful harvest is not, however, a tactical objective or a specific goal. It is a good intention, the purpose of the activity, but it does not point to a specific measurable target. Distinguishing between the concepts of broad purposes and clear goals is critical. At the operational level, it is goals that are being worked out. Why these are being undertaken is the task of those setting the strategy.

Some find goals difficult to write down; it gets easier with practice! Others are afraid to define them too specifically in case they fail. However, if your goal is to see your congregation grow from 100 to 150 in the coming year, there is a great difference between achieving 149 people or only 101. With the first everyone would say, 'You virtually succeeded'. With the second they might ask, 'What assumptions did you have? One or more of these was not correct.' This would help to identify the cause of the problem and so give the chance of setting a more realistic goal for the planning of next year's growth.

It has sometimes been suggested that setting goals is unscriptural. Jesus, however, had specific measurable targets. He was determined to reach Jerusalem, for example, and actually said to some friendly Pharisees who warned him to move on as Herod wanted to kill Him, 'Go tell that fox, "I will drive out demons and heal people today and tomorrow and on the third day *I will reach my goal.*"'[4]

The Seventh-Day Adventists are one of the smaller world-wide denominations. At the beginning of the 1990s, their international headquarters asked every single congregation throughout the world how many people they would baptise each year between 1990 and 1995. They themselves set a target of 2.6 million, worked out as a person every minute! When all the churches had given their estimates, their 'faith goals', as they were described, the total came to 2.9 million. After these five years were over, I was interested to know how well they had succeeded, and so wrote to the President of the British Union Conference at their UK headquarters in Watford. He was kind enough to send me details. The combined world-wide total had been 3.1 million. Never say that goals don't work! They enable challenges to be met.

A key word used in this description of tactical objectives is 'measurable'. This is what distinguishes goals from purposes. Goals can always be measured, either in terms of quantity, time, or people involved. In some time

management books the characteristics of good goals are
summarised as being SMART:

S pecific

M easurable

A chievable

R ealistic

T imed

All these are useful in defining the objectives that need to
be reached or worked out. 'Timed' means a date or time is
set for accomplishing it, so that you will know at some time
in the future whether or not you have reached your goal.
The time may be a few hours or days away, but often it is
weeks, months or even years. In terms of tactical objectives,
though, we are probably not thinking of periods much
longer than one or two years.

Robert Schuller, who built the Crystal Cathedral in Los
Angeles, once said, 'When you set no goals for growth,
you set your goals for no growth.' Goals and growth
go together. You want growth? Set some goals! Identify
specific measurable objectives to aim at.

Establishing priorities

Do you ever find you have too much to do? Most leaders in
business and church life will heartily agree! As someone
once joked, 'The only person who ever got his work done
by Friday was Robinson Crusoe!'

The word directly under 'goals' in Table 4.1 is 'priorities'.
The ability to establish which job should be done next
and which after that is an important management ability.
Some people dither, fluster when asked to do too many
things and find themselves unable to see the wood for

the trees. Others, often women, are able to multi-task, somehow able to do several things simultaneously. We would all like PAs like that! Yet others put things in a firm order and do the first job first, followed by the second and third, and so on. Others do a bit of task one, a bit of task two and a bit of task three, thus keeping all three balls in the air, so to speak. It doesn't really matter how we learn to cope; some comments on pressure were given in the previous chapter.

Priorities, like plans, come in one of two ways (or both!) – is it a conflict of too many things to do, or is it the pressure of too little time to do it? The *value* of what you are doing may also be important, as well as the *position* of the person for whom you are doing it. If the person wanting you to do something is your boss, or Chair, or someone highly respected by you, you are more likely to want to do his/ her job first.

If you try to rethink your priorities, you will need to include everything you do in that process. Home and family priorities, work and church priorities, personal and leisure priorities will all need to go into the same bowl for mixing and sorting. You can't do one part without the other.

Spiritual priorities are a critical part of the equation for church leaders and Christian people. There are three things that you cannot delegate to anyone else – your walk with God, the position you hold in your particular family and your vision. If you are very busy you may ask your husband or wife to pray *for* you; you cannot ask him/her to pray *instead* of you! It is all too easy in the pressure of life to allow your time with God, however and whenever that may normally be, to slip in the pressures of the moment. Actually, God misses our contact with Him; one of the complaints made through the prophets in the Old

Testament is that God's people took Him for granted and simply ignored Him. Jesus said 'I have called you friends' – and friends usually talk to each other and spend time with each other if the relationship is to flourish and not stagnate!

There is a fairly easy way to resolve multiple short-term priorities. It is called the ABC technique, although more accurately it should be the ACB Technique. Write down all the things you have to do. This is a good practice anyway, whether you are stretched or not. The back of an envelope, a new sheet of paper, or a list supplied with a diary specially for the purpose – it doesn't matter. Nor does it matter when you do it – last thing at night, ready for tomorrow, or first thing in the morning.

Go through your list looking for those items to be labelled A – the things that must be done, have the highest value, are the most important. Then go through the list again and identify the Cs – least important, lowest value, can be left for today. Everything not an A or a C is a B. If you have too many As, this is normal! Go through the As and mark them AA or AB or AC. Then start work with the AAs, go on to the ABs and ACs. Should you finish all those, go for the Bs. The next day, re-establish your priorities; you may find some of the Bs have become As or the Cs should now be Bs.

A longer and more thorough way of handling multiple long-term priorities is to identify which are (a) of low importance and which are (b) of high importance. Likewise, identify which are (c) of low urgency and which are (d) of high urgency. Those of high urgency but of low importance as far as you personally are concerned can be delegated to someone else, if there is such a person. Those of low urgency but high importance can be put into the diary as something to be planned in detail then.

However, the majority of items will fall into the high importance and great urgency box. Divide these into four groups as shown in Figure 7.1:

Table 7.1
Items of high urgency and great importance

Urgency / Importance	Short Term	Long Term
Minor	Z	Y
Major	Y	X

Items of major importance and long-term significance (Xs) should be undertaken first. Whether one then does short-term items of major importance or long-term items of less value is debatable, but both come before short-term items of minor importance. You follow X–Y–Z in this diagram. There is, however, an alternative description for 'X' – it is the word 'vision'. Ultimately it is your vision that drives your priorities, your passion and your push for accomplishment. In the crux, military strategic thinking depends on visionary objectives!

Agreeing the timing of events
Having identified the specific measurable goals that are to be undertaken and put these into an appropriate priority order, it is usually not too difficult to agree with your colleagues the times for completion for these various events.

The value of such agreement is that then the list can be circulated, so that everyone knows who is doing what, and where and when. This communication process is vital for team harmony and efficient operation.

Tactical level

The tactical success level is the practical part. It is where the rubber hits the road. It is the sharp end of performance. It is the nitty gritty of action.

In a business, the CEO will be responsible for the strategic level; his/her department heads for the operational level; those working in a specific department for the tactical success. How a telephone is answered makes a direct impact on the image of a firm. How accurately data are entered into a computer is vital for future trading or analysis. How neatly letters are typed and how quickly queries are answered will determine the public's opinion of a company. The most sophisticated strategy can be let down at the tactical level. That is why the word attached to it – 'success' – is a crucial addition.

It is similar in a church context. The minister may work out a strategy that the Council or deacons accept. He/she may have a youth worker, or an administrator, and perhaps an assistant. There is probably a treasurer. Those teaching in the Sunday school, under the overall direction of the youth worker, are critical in the forming of a relationship with the children. If the administrator gets the week's notices wrong, the efficiency of the whole church looks odd. If the assistant asks someone to lead in prayer and he/she doesn't turn up for that service, the worship is let down. Those at the sharp end are in many ways more obvious than those determining objectives. Without them, the whole church can grind to a halt. Chiefs and Indians are both needed, but especially the Indians!

The tactical level, therefore, is not just part of the whole, but the vital ingredient that makes everything else work. It is essential that these nuts and bolts get clear, great and constant attention.

Tactical and operational training

Allocating a training fund towards tactical success there-fore seems sensible. There are many specialist trainers providing courses on how to teach a Sunday school class, how to prepare talks, how to welcome people into a church, how to prepare a newsletter or magazine, how to use a computer, etc., and the myriad activities in a church context that come under 'tactical'. Some of the training can be internal. There are organisations that specialise in certain types of activity, like bereavement counselling. Local Social Service departments can sometimes help with training. If your church doesn't yet have a training budget, would it be worth adding one in for next year? In a church setting, it may, of course, be cheaper to use any in your congregation who already have secular training in the skills needed, if you have such people!

Training at the operational level is usually done at a specialist or college level. A children's or youth worker will be expected to have some relevant qualification. An assistant minister will often have been to theological college. A good church secretary will often have relevant experience. Such training is not usually internal, and often is paid for either personally or through central church funds. Large businesses or the Civil Service may pay for a few special personnel to get training of this type, but normally heads of department come ready-made for the job.

Strategic training

Training in strategic thinking is very rare in church circles. There are places like the Henley Centre or the Chartered Management Institute offering relevant courses, but the cost of these is high, so generally only the largest agencies or businesses will pay for their people to go on them. If, however, secular organisations find this kind of training useful, should not the churches consider such also?

In the Armed Forces there is the Combined Services Staff College, which helps to train potential senior officers both in strategic thinking and military doctrine over a three-month intensive course. Established less than 15 years ago by the then Chief of the General Staff, Field Marshal Sir Nigel Bagnall, there is now no Admiral, General or Air Marshal who has not been through it. While the high command therefore may not always think with one mind, they do have a united way to think strategically. That surely is of crucial importance for the welfare of our country.

Cannot the church do likewise? We seek to serve a higher Sovereign than our royal family, important though the Queen is. Could not senior leaders follow a common course teaching focusing on the ability to do, and concepts of, strategic thinking? This seems to be of overwhelming importance, a critical long-term objective, and something well worth funding from some of the monies available to the most senior church leaders.

If such could be undertaken it should be available to all those who, in Church of England terminology, are likely to become Archdeacons, Deans of Cathedrals, and Suffragan or Diocesan Bishops. Indeed, one could almost say, as in the Armed Forces and as with head teachers in schools, a person should not be considered for promotion *unless* he/she has attended the Staff College or taken the Head Teachers' qualification.

Training does already exist for those newly appointed as Archdeacons, both as a short course and over their initial induction into the actual job, but it is not mandatory. To be fair, training is also given to newly appointed Bishops, but this tends to be on a one-by-one level, and/or through a small mentor group. While doubtless valuable, this is far removed from the concept of a Staff College focusing on culture and strategy.

It might well be argued, with the responsibility for larger churches growing, that those asked to take the senior leadership of these should likewise have attended a Staff College or something similar.[5]

Three levels of thinking and leadership

Three different levels of operation have been described – strategic, operational and tactical. All are important and essential to the whole. The omission of one, or a weak link, would cause the ultimate objective to fail. Vision depends critically on the infrastructure for successful fulfilment.

Three levels of thinking

The word 'thinking' has frequently been associated with 'strategic' in this book. However, thinking is also essential for the operational and tactical modes. There is no suggestion that the top person does all the thinking for everyone! However, the *type* of thinking undertaken by each level is different, which may or may not relate to intelligence.

- *Strategic thinking* has to be wide ranging; outside the box; spanning past and present; lateral thinking; moving into the future.

- *Operational thinking* relates to specific areas of management responsibility; it is functional; broad but specific; delegating detailed responsibility to others.

- *Tactical thinking* is detailed, practical, day to day, at ground level. It is worked out in the rush of circumstances, usually without great reflection. It is the thinking of the chase, the thrill of adventure, the actions to be taken as situations unfold.

The training officer thinks in one way, the treasurer in another and the communications person in yet another, but all think operationally, professionally in respect to their specific responsibilities. Likewise in a church setting: the youth officer has age group concerns; the assistant minister teaching and communication needs; the church secretary probably needs to work and think both on a day-to-day and week-by-week timeframe. This is all operational thinking.

The house group leader is concerned for his/her group in a pastoral and friendship way; the worship leader thinks about music and atmosphere and how people can feel the wind of the Spirit; the minister taking a wedding this week focuses on the happy couple and what their future may hold, and how to help strangers understand the service. Quite different types of thinking, but all within the general remit of tactical thinking, which is practical, relevant, a day at a time.

Three levels of leadership

All those involved in this process are *leaders*. Tactical thinking is just as real and important as strategic thinking; it may operate in a different plane, but it is not less relevant. Operational thinking translates the strategic thinking into practice; just as a glove needs a hand inside it, so too these two work intimately together.

- *Strategic leadership* is where it all begins.
- *Operational leadership* is where the vision is made to happen.

- *Tactical leadership* is facilitating others through a challenging, comforting, or continuing process.

All are types of leadership, and if training is important for one group it is for them all. The process of appointment is relevant also, how long it is for, and how each person is evaluated. Is there a job description for each? It is amazing how many tasks in a church context, even at senior level, have no job description! What are the expectations that go with each position? To whom is each responsible? How is that responsibility exercised? Are there any financial elements? If so, how are these accounted for? Can expenses be claimed? If so, how? Might training be necessary? Is this task a step towards another job? How might this job impact the home and/or family life of the person concerned? How long is it for? How many hours a week are expected? Is there any kind of security risk? Does the person have to be vetted, internally or externally? Have we been biased in terms of age, gender, race or physical ability in the making of this appointment? How will any grievances be aired, and how handled? Who has the authority to make this appointment?

Many of these kinds of questions are not even considered in a church context when someone is asked to help out here or there. However, in today's modern world, these types of questions become more and more important, and some have legal implications.

This type of division of leadership has not originated with the Military Model of strategic thinking. Others have used similar divisions. One such calls them, respectively, Senior, Associate and Local. A group in the United States called them Senior, Ministry and Discipling. However, whatever the terminology, the type of leadership and especially the type of thinking that each undertakes is not altered.

The operational impact level

In his lecture, General Dannatt described the Operational Impact Level in more detail, indicating that it had three components to make it truly effective. These sets of activities are all related, and would probably need to be developed together for maximum efficiency.

Deep Operations

'Deep Operations are those things that we need to do to shape the situation to our overall advantage.'[6] Information is a key part of this, and so is planning. Taking a preliminary survey to ascertain attitudes or identify key aspects of how others are thinking is also part of deep operations. In military terms it could, for example, include long-range pre-emptive aircraft strikes; presumably the Mohne Dam broken by Barnes Wallace's bouncing bomb, dropped by Guy Gibson, in the Second World War would be classified as a deep operation since it certainly impacted the situation to the Allied advantage.

In church terms it means trying to understand:

- What do those who are likely to disagree with this project or policy actually find objectionable? Why do they feel that? How can these objections best be overcome? (Is it the Local Authority or an internal committee who are opposed to an extension, for instance? Are their objections based on legal or cultural grounds?)

- Are there some things that need to be made public so that everyone can understand better why it is we are suggesting this way of proceeding? (Many people's private lives have been exposed in the media; are Christians' private lives and personal views relevant in this context?)

- Who are the decision-makers? Who are the people who exercise a crucial influence over them? How can these people best be reached, and in what way? (Newspaper headlines on the day of national elections are often thought to sway uncertain voters; would large-scale publicity help our cause? When huge numbers of billboards carried posters advertising Alpha courses in September 1998 they prompted thousands of enquiries on the part of the public and many courses began as a consequence.)

- Is there a series of actions that need to be taken over an extended period of time in order to persuade opinion? (A number of organisations planned events over several years in order to persuade the Synod of the Church of England that women should be ordained.)

- What information do we not have? Is it possible to get it? What is the best way of obtaining it, and from whom? (Several Christian organisations wanting specific information for commercial, theological or extension reasons have commissioned Christian Research to obtain that information for them.)

Such questions cannot be answered lightly, and require clear and sustained strategic thought. What are the objectives being sought? Not only how do we reach those objectives (or fulfil the vision), but how do we persuade people that reaching them in this way is the best path to follow? Much discussion will need to take place; members of the team will need to play their part very carefully. This is where 'iron sharpens iron'[7] and everyone prays much for wisdom! Deep operations require much prayer.

Close Operations

Close operations are the day-to-day actions that have to take place to ensure something will happen. A Sunday school teacher has to know what story is to be taught next week, will need to be able to resource any visual aids that are suggested and find time to prepare any items that will be handed out. Close operations are those tasks that have to be done to make whatever it is happen.

In more complex circumstances, such as the holding of a holiday club during the next Easter holiday for children living in the neighbourhood of the church, close operations will require getting enough helpers, working through the programme, arranging publicity, ensuring enough finance is available, making sure the room where it is being held is, or can be made, suitable, etc. Arrangements also need to be made for welcoming the children, dealing with anxious parents, thinking about follow-up when it is over.

Many people would simply call this detailed planning, and in many ways it is. It can be done individually if necessary, though for bigger tasks a team is required, since the work becomes too much for one person. It can be called anything, but this is simply a marker to indicate that this kind of immediate and careful preparation is essential if any project is to succeed. The macro impact is built up of micro items, thoroughly worked out.

Spiritually, close operations require a constant walk with God. We need to hear His voice, and to do things His way. The WWJD armbands that many now wear remind one of this: 'What Would Jesus Do?' The question was the subtitle of a book originally published in 1897[8] but indicates how 'close operations' can continue today.

Rear Operations

Rear operations are probably second nature to most people in the Armed Forces, but are hardly ever considered in church circles. 'Rear operations are those things which we need to do to protect ourselves, to sustain ourselves logistically and to ensure that we have a reserve available to react to the unexpected.'[9] In other words, don't start something if you can't carry it through! That applies also to our personal Christian activities!

Protect ourselves
From April 2002 the Charity Commissioners have had the power to investigate charities. It is far better to ensure that you are doing everything that you should, rather than wait for an inspection to reveal what you are doing wrong! What do 'we need to do to protect ourselves'? This is especially important as new criteria come in from the European Union or other sources in such areas as child protection, for instance. Far, far better to take action and introduce additional administrative procedures than to allow a catastrophe to occur.

Saga is a well-known company focusing on activities especially for those aged 50 and over. Holidays were arranged to tour various parts of China in the summer of 2003, but with the SARS epidemic raging earlier that year, they were all cancelled. Saga's business would have suffered hugely had a client died of the illness. They were simply protecting themselves.

Sustain ourselves
Unfortunately this has not always been church or agency experience. In 1995 Christian Research published the first of what was planned to be ten regional volumes of the *UK Christian Schools Book*. But we failed to ensure it was something that the schools concerned felt was really helpful for them. Sales were so poor that the project was abandoned.

It cost Holy Trinity, Brompton a large amount of money to advertise the Alpha course so publicly in 1998. It worked, but Alpha works best if it is repeated. Could they find such money again? But the plans for that process had been

considered before the 1998 experience. 'If it works, will
we be able to repeat it?' With an affirmative answer, they
could risk the 1998 appeal, and so went ahead. They were
able to 'sustain themselves logistically'.

Reserves available
There are always occasions when one has to risk everything.
If something goes wrong, there are no reserves available.
One Christian organisation had a brilliant photographer
who was capable of producing extremely effective and
heart-rending pictures. It didn't think it worthwhile for
him to have an assistant. Tragically he was killed in an air
crash off the Kenyan coast; it took them some years to find
someone else, and even so, he wasn't quite as good.

No reserve was available. There are many such stories
in the history of Christian mission.

Actually having reserves can cost money, time and effort.
Many may have to be persuaded that it is a valuable thing
to do. It can be frustrating to those in the reserve if they are
not actually used. But the purpose of having reserves is so
that there can be little loss in momentum if the unexpected
happens. It can be argued that they are equally involved in
the Lord's battle and that it can ebb and flow, as He directs.
Yes it can, and does, but not to take advantage of a crucial
opportunity when you have it may require years of further
effort to make up the ground thus lost.

On one occasion, some of David's men were too tired to
fight, so he left them with the baggage (1 Sam. 30:10), that
is, gave them alternative reserve deployment. They shared
equally, however, in the spoils of battle (verse 24).

Identifying what reserves there ought to be is no more
than working through the 'risk assessment' that many
agencies are now legally required to undertake. Identifying
the risks and putting a probability of likely occurrence

against each is a useful exercise. Sometimes some risks are too great; what reserve plans need to be established to cover that contingency? Careful thought and strategic assessment are required.

The centre of gravity

There was one other important component of strategic thinking that General Dannatt mentioned in his lecture. This was the concept of 'Centre of Gravity'. This may be defined as:

> That essential action or actions which if carried out successfully will allow and enable the fulfilment of strategic, operational and tactical objectives.

In other words, the Centre of Gravity is at the heart of success, what in Chapters 1 and 3 was referred to as following the invisible.

Richard Dannatt gave an actual example from the 1994 Bosnian campaign in which the British Army was asked to disarm the two warring sides. The General in charge, General Sir Michael Rose, decided that the Centre of Gravity in this case was to persuade the Bosnian people that it was better to take the negotiated peace settlement offered through the United Nations, and thus live in peace, rather than to continue fighting each other for their varying objectives.[10] In order to achieve this, the General and other senior members of the Army High Command went and visited individual villages, talking with the local people and their leaders directly. It took a long time to talk through the options, but eventually the invisible hope for peace proved stronger than the visible fighting, and the General and his colleagues won the day.

Baptist example

We were asked to lead a strategy day for a Kent Baptist church situated near a school, but up a relatively unused road. We asked the congregation, 'What does this church have to do in order to make the community want to come to your church?' In other words, what is the invisible Centre of Gravity that would enable your visions of outreach to be fulfilled?

The Elders were separated off as a group, as were the Sunday school teachers and other operational leaders. The remainder broke up into age groups.

The older people knew what they needed. 'Older people on this estate need to know that the church cares. A coffee morning once a week would be a sure way of encouraging them to come, and maybe it would turn into a luncheon club eventually.'

Those in their more middle years were equally clear. 'Most homes in this area have two working parents. If we provided an after-school club to look after the children when they come out of the school opposite until their parents can collect them after work finishes, we would have a flourishing club. It would certainly pay for itself, and provide an excellent opportunity to encourage the parents and children to come on Sunday as well.'

The young people (under 25) were very clear what had to happen also. 'We need to have a youth service on Saturday evening, not Sunday morning. It needs to be café-style, with tables and food and drink, and to have a good Christian band. Give us that, and we guarantee to fill this church.' I am sure they would have done, too!

We asked the other two groups for their suggestions. The Sunday school teachers' group had none at all, and nor had the Elders! The latter said they were considering if it was appropriate to use the church premises for any activity that did not allow the direct presentation of the Gospel at every opportunity!

It was clear that the opportunity was unlikely to be taken. Three good suggestions were almost certain to be squandered by the leadership. Without that Centre of Gravity their plans for outreach would be most unlikely to be successful. They could not see the invisible.

Alpha courses

In the four years 1994 to 1997, 400,000 people attended Alpha courses throughout the UK. However, in the next four years, 1998 to 2001, the number attending was over 900,000 people, a number aided and sustained by the huge advertising campaign that took place in the September of each of the latter four years promising 'an Alpha course in a church near you'. The businesspeople in the Committee behind the Alpha course were very shrewd. How could they continue the progress already seen through the mid–1990s?

By moving beyond individual local churches to the public at large, the target audience, they helped to create a demand for the courses to which the churches responded by supplying them. Normal means of attracting people to the courses through personal invitation, Alpha Supper Initiatives, were fine, but the Centre of Gravity was in establishing a felt need in many of the non-Christian public for the course. This invisible component, the felt need, helped to create the course's success.

A political example

In July 2002 Theresa May was appointed Chair of the Conservative Party. In an editorial giving its congratulations, the *Daily Telegraph*[11] observed that in the 2001

General Election the Tories had seen a slight swing in their direction, but that this had not yielded the 30 seats the party should have gained in Parliament because the gains were in the seats already held. 'Most of your campaigning energies are concentrated in your heartland areas,' it said. Similar comments might be made about the church!

The writer then proceeded to give some strategic suggestions that it was thought the new Chair might like to consider:

- The time has come to give substance to national membership. It is ridiculous that you still have to rely on your local associations to tell you who and where your members are.

- The same applies to financial resources. As long as membership subscriptions are going chiefly to wealthy (and safe) constituencies, you will find it difficult to break out of your rural and suburban base.

- You need a new style of canvassing: one designed to win elections rather than please your activists. You must target non-Tories, and not simply canvass to find out where your existing support is.

- Learn from the way American parties operate, with highly sophisticated forms of profiling and direct mailing. Your local committee structure has barely changed since the 1950s.

- Make sure your MPs are working in neighbouring marginals, rather than simply grooming their own majorities. You may want to formalise this through the whips' office.

Not all these ideas will be popular in the short term. Some of your activists will resent being told to change. But this, surely, is the time to persuade them; and you are ideally placed to do it.

These comments, with simple amendments in terminology, could be applied not only to other political parties, but to other institutions like the church! Look nationally not locally; put money where growth is essential; target those outside; learn from others; ensure leaders are reaching outsiders. These are key strategies. Putting them into practice, as the editorial also recognises, may not be quite so easy!

There is also an obvious Centre of Gravity component behind these strategies: winning the next election! Playing to win is vital, and is considered in the final chapter.

An agency example

SAO Cambodia works, as its name suggests, in south-east Asia. Begun through the stimulus of Major Chhirc Taing in 1973, who later died in Cambodia, it continues to help Cambodians spiritually, socially and through development projects. At its April 2002 national Conference, the question was posed, 'What does SAO Cambodia have to do to earn the right to represent Cambodia to British churches?'

Answers to this Centre of Gravity question were:

- Document its ongoing work
- Upgrade the amount of spiritual work being done in Cambodia
- Have some Khmer authority on the Council
- Let a Khmer pastor tour the UK under the auspices of SAO Cambodia
- Establish relationships between UK and Khmer Christians
- Organise more 'visit Cambodia' trips for UK Christians
- Tell of its past successes, showing it already has a proven ability and track record

- Be a resource centre for Cambodia by supplying information about the country
- Seek more partnership opportunities in new or existing projects
- Become more visual/visible to UK churches.

SAO Cambodia has been faithfully working through this list since that Conference, with some success. Such a list of answers may well come from like questions asked in similar circumstances. The answers, however, are not Centre of Gravity answers. As a Trustee of SAO Cambodia, I was part of the process, and therefore can take part of the blame. While they are useful answers for current activity, the real Centre of Gravity answers to the question require deeper, longer and more careful thought.

This is in no sense to disparage or discourage SAO Cambodia. I can testify from personal experience the excellent quality of their work. But this example is given to illustrate that Centre of Gravity questions are not easily or quickly answered, and are most unlikely to be a shopping list of activities. These have their place – but that place is in the visible outworkings of a strategy, not the invisible purposes behind it. The Centre of Gravity is more concerned with what can't be seen than what can.

Staying in business

In their book *Strategic Church Leadership*[12] Robin Gill and Derek Burke ask the question 'What do we *have* to do to stay in business?' This question has nothing whatever to do with commercial business, but rather thinking of 'business' as 'retaining a sense of identity and purpose for the institution', or, perhaps, enabling the organisation to continue and fulfil its vision.

Part of the answer is to have a vision and a strategy for fulfilling it. Part of that fulfilment lies in identifying the invisible component, the Centre of Gravity, which, if successfully completed, will create the conditions for allowing the strategy to be fulfilled. In other words, the Centre of Gravity is not an optional extra, take it or leave it. It is the core to what has to be done if everything else is to work out. It is the invisible to which strategic thinking must rise and define.

Spades!

This is the Military Model, depicted by a well-used tool. Precise, forward marching, clear. First your strategic vision, then the operational process, with its deep, close and rear components, and the careful strategic planning required for each part. Finally, tactical success, upon which all depends. Behind it though, like the pillar of cloud that covered the tabernacle by day and the appearance of fire by night,[13] is the panoply of the Centre of Gravity, the invisible goal that makes or breaks a project.

Deliberate, weighed strategic thinking is essential for this entire mode of working. And for that you need strategic leadership. To this key topic we now turn in the final chapter.

Notes

[1] Major General Richard Dannatt CBE MC, *Training Leaders to Think Strategically* (London: Christian Research, April 2002).

[2] Ibid., p. 7.

[3] This was the average church income for churches in England in 2000, as given in Peter Brierley (ed.), *Religious Trends* No. 4, 2003/2004 (London: Christian Research, 2003), Figure 5.2.1.

[4] Luke 13:32 NIV, my italics.

[5] Christian Research facilitated an initial Staff College for leaders of larger Anglican churches (usual Sunday attendance 350 or more) for a week in June 2003, and has organised others since.

[6] Dannatt, *Training Leaders to Think Strategically*, p. 19.

[7] Proverbs 27:17.

[8] Charles Sheldon, *In His Steps: What Would Jesus Do?* (London: George Routledge & Sons, 1897).

[9] Dannatt, *Training Leaders to Think Strategically*, p. 20.

[10] Ibid., p. 11.

[11] *Daily Telegraph*, 29th July 2002.

[12] Professor Robin Gill and Vice-Chancellor Derek Burke, *Strategic Church Leadership* (London: SPCK, 1996).

[13] Numbers 9:16.

Chapter 8

Playing to Win

Strategic leadership is essential if we are playing to win. This chapter looks not at strategic planning, about which many books have been written,[1] but at strategic leadership. Strategic thinking and planning accomplish nothing if there is no strategic leadership to make them effective.

General Charles Gordon once asked Li Hung Chang, an old Chinese leader, 'What is leadership? And how is humanity divided?' He received this cryptic answer: 'There are only three kinds of people in the world – those that are movable, those that are immovable, and those that move them.'[2] Strategic leaders are in the third category.

If leadership is about moving people – and situations – then what part does strategic thinking and vision play in that process? A leader has to know what he/she is aiming for (the vision or the strategic objective) or, in other words, what movement or change he/she believes is necessary. Only then can the actual movement begin. An earlier book on strategic leadership[3] described that movement in four ways: Planning, Activating, Motivating and Evaluating. All these are indeed essential, but in this book we have been considering more the kick-start processes by the leader rather than the precise mechanisms.

We have considered four processes, and it is worth briefly revisiting them:

- ♣ Clubs, Vision Building, is a logical progressive method of moving towards the immediate future, which many leaders with the ability to work towards shorter-term or smaller (but nevertheless challenging) visions will use.

- ♦ Diamonds, Horizon Mission Methodology, is an imaginative values-based process for thinking backwards from a (distant) future position, which those with creative ability will probably find easier to adopt than others.

- ♥ Hearts, Relating and Delegating, works well for those exceptional people-people who not only see an opportunity but also have the ability to recognise its importance.

- ♠ Spades, the Military Model, looks at a strategic objective in great detail. This works well with those who like detail, but the crux of this method is for those who have an invisible overarching strategic objective to accomplish and the ability to fulfil it.

All these methods are relevant in their different contexts, and according to the characteristics of individual leaders. They are based on different approaches to thinking future: Clubs is a vision-centred approach, Diamonds is values centred, Hearts is more people centred, and Spades excellence centred.[4] Each of the above descriptions deliberately contains the word 'ability'.

There are various aspects of ability, including those mentioned in Chapter 1: personality, current situation and past experience, the people in your team. One aspect of ability that Meredith Belbin raised is worth looking at in more detail. He said that a successful team needs people with a range of intelligences.

Intelligence

Discussions relating intelligence and leadership are less common in the general management literature. The word is usually equated to a person's 'IQ', or Intelligence Quotient, a figure that can be worked out through various tests. To join the organisation Mensa, for example, you have to have an IQ of at least 148 on the Cattell B test scale or gain a percentile score of 98% on various tests, which puts you in the top 2% of the population. The norm is 100, and 95% of the population are between 80 and 120. Pupils in the upper streams of secondary school, and those admitted to grammar schools, usually have an IQ on the Mensa scale in excess of 110 or 115. As a measure it is doubtless a useful summary in some situations, but the public image (though not strictly in the way it is usually worked out) is that intelligence is only about having factual and logical knowledge. 'Intelligence' undoubtedly does include these, but as the management author Charles Handy has pointed out, it is much more than that.

In his book *The Hungry Spirit*[5] he lists 11 types of intelligence, although he explains that the theory originated with Howard Gardner of Harvard University. These types are as follows, together with one that he omits:

- **Factual** intelligence, the ability to remember and reproduce facts on a wide range of topics. In the extreme, the kind of person who wins *Mastermind* or the radio 'Brain of Britain' quiz.

- **Analytic** intelligence, or the ability to be logical, having powers of reasoning. Combined with Factual intelligence, such people did well in the older types of examinations.

- **Numerate** intelligence, the ability to understand numbers, and sometimes having the agility of recall or the capacity to interpret and explain their meaning.

- **Spatial** intelligence, the ability that artists and many entrepreneurs (like Richard Branson) have. They are people who can see patterns in things, and often make excellent systems analysts. The best computer people have this type of intelligence, understanding implicitly how many windows[6] can operate simultaneously.

- **Linguistic** intelligence, or the ability with languages. Handy rather unkindly says that if a person only has this intelligence all it means is that 'he will speak nonsense in 8 languages'!

- **Musical** intelligence, the ability to read, play and hear music and understand and interpret its meanings and moods.

- **Practical** intelligence, frequently called 'common sense', or 'moral imagination' (by C.S. Lewis),[7] is the ability to understand how to do things around the home, in the office or wherever. People with this intelligence are essential for running any church, business or organisation! It seems to me that often women who are homemakers bringing up children have this kind of intelligence.

- **Athletic** intelligence, the ability to know how your body works physically and what it can do, and how to help it do it.

- **Intuitive** intelligence, the ability to empathise, which Handy suggests is often particularly something that handicapped people have. It is the ability to sense and see what is not immediately obvious.

- **Interpersonal** intelligence, or perhaps social intelligence, the ability 'to get things done with and through other people'.

- **Emotional** intelligence (about which whole books have been written), the ability to be self-aware, in self-control, with persistence, zeal and self-motivation. It is recognising the impact we have on others. This is but one feature of the many psychometric tests which are often used by companies and institutions to assess people and which are generally available on the Internet.[8]

- **Spiritual** intelligence, the one that Handy omits, but, as any Christian leader will know, the ability that some have to perceive and apply spiritual values.

Handy makes it clear that no one will have all of these types of intelligence, but that everyone will probably have one. Most people probably have four or five types. It should also be stated that the above list is not in some kind of 'order'; there is no implied suggestion that certain types of intelligence are somehow more important than other types. It will also be true that some people will think they have an intelligence they don't!

In terms of strategic leadership, however, it is worth asking which of these types the leader him/herself has, and which the members of his/her team.

The *value* of such an analysis Belbin brings out in his book.[9] He makes two key observations about intelligence with respect to management teams. The first of these is that unsuccessful teams too often have similar types or levels of intelligence. If you have only PhDs in your team, it is likely to be deficient in a number of areas!

The second point he makes is the reverse of the first, but he feels the issue so important that he identifies the two separately. Winning teams will have a range of intelligences within it. That range may well be across the types Handy has identified as well as across the IQ range.

Before Margaret Thatcher sought to abolish social class distinctions, we talked about the upper class, the middle class and the working class. There was an implied hierarchy in this terminology – the upper class was above the middle class and the middle class above the working class, and in terms of the average income each class generally earned or inherited that hierarchy was correct! In terms of the intelligence of each class, however, the hierarchy was definitely NOT true. Each class may typically have had different types of intelligence, but one kind of intelligence is not superior to another. It is far too easy to misjudge people's capability: Mark Pemberton,

Business Director of English Heritage, for example, was once a litter collector.[10]

One energetic Baptist church in North London with many attenders from different ethnic communities has recently started a second morning service, as it was unable comfortably to accommodate everyone who came. The senior pastor, however, has found no one in his congregations able to write good minutes of meetings, and he has to do these himself. His deacons have the intelligence to grow the church, but not this ability. It must not be presumed that only certain types of intelligence are needed to have a winning team, or to exercise strategic leadership.

In other words, part of successful strategic leadership is in the balancing of one's team, knowing individual gifts or intelligences, and then *playing to win deliberately using those strengths.* This kind of knowledge is critical for winning players. Without it, you will not be successful. Your team will make you or thwart you. That is equally true in a church, a Christian organisation or a secular business context.

It also means that strategic leadership is a team affair, not a solo occupation. Leaders who walk alone don't lead; they are simply walking! Leaders are marked by the ability to take other people with them. *Leadership is a Team Sport* is the title of a chapter in one of George Barna's books.[11]

Generations

Of all the factors outlined in the context described in Chapter 2, the generational differences are perhaps the most important, shown in part by the variations in Belbin types by age in Table 1.4. A strategic leader is able to work with people of all ages and to recognise their gifts. One

Christian organisation took on a school leaver with little experience and whose speaking grammar was often incorrect. She had failed to find a job with anyone else. She proved a model worker, dedicated, enthusiastic, willing to tackle any job, and was still happily with them (and they with her) four years later.

Generation Xers and Boomers

One of the features of the so-called Generation X generation (broadly those in their 20s and 30s at the start of the 21st century) is that their thinking tends to be creative and technological[12] rather than linear or logical. They have other values also: they respect openness rather than status, and will tend to look at the team with whom they will be working more than the actual job to be done.[13]

Generation Xers 'have had their approach to leaders and leadership moulded by a set of postmodern world view presuppositions that are by definition the very opposite of the modern world view of their seniors'.[14] The same author, Peter Stephenson, an engineer church planter in Spain, continues:

> The antagonism between leaders and young people is particularly marked between the Boomer generation [broadly those in their 40s and 50s at the beginning of the century] and Generation X. It was the spectacular aggressively self-confident can-do attitude of the Boomers that led to economic boom in the latter part of the twentieth century. But this same boom has caused global environmental destruction, and has been paid for by exploitation of the non-Western world and the emotional suffering of a generation of children whose parents placed a higher premium on their own personal freedom and success than on their offspring's need for a safe and secure family environment. And as if this were not enough, much of the Boomers' success was in their ability to harness and use the skills of their juniors.[15]

He quotes George Barna, an American researcher, who wrote:

> Boomers sought to gain control of the decision-making apparatus from day one, intent upon redefining authority, burying tradition, and increasing their profile in business and government. The arrival of the Boomers signalled the end of predictability, the rule of fairness and the notion of the common good ... The Boomers had a single goal: to win on their own terms ... Boomers believed in the entrepreneurial way of life, but the irony is that the most successful Boomer entrepreneurs were those who cashed in on the technological breakthroughs developed by the Gen Xers.[16]

Work practices in the 21st century

These are tough words, and some Christian leaders will feel they are over-exaggerated to make a point. Perhaps they are, but the point is nevertheless real. Strategic leaders understand that one of the key energies of Generation Xers is their concern for integrity; they often have an uncanny ability to spot invisible agendas and hypocrisy. Generation Xers often work hard (even while travelling, in hotels, planes and cyber cafés), but they *work to live*, a complete reversal of the Boomer work ethic.[17]

A key difference between the work practice of Generation Xers and Boomers is summarised by two 'management-speak' sets of letters: MBO and MBP. Boomers worked with MBO: Management by Objectives, working towards goals they or their leaders had set. This defined a whole work culture, some of which was worked out in detail in the previous chapter.

MBP, on the other hand, Management by Project, helps to epitomise what Generation Xers prefer. Projects do not assume long-term employment with one employer, but they provide valuable experience (training) through their completion, and they require sustained team effort over a given period for a particular purpose. One can see why the Relating and Delegating model can sometimes produce spectacular results. If, however, we use the word 'vision' for 'project', it becomes apparent that strategic thinking relates very much to the contemporary ways of working. What your vision is cannot be just an esoteric question, but rather is the critical process of moving towards the future. For Generation Xers the big risk is that some will not wish to follow the vision of the leader, and so holding the team together becomes more difficult.

This agrees with the argument of author David Cannon, who says that 'today's young graduates want work that is interesting and not just well paid. They will gravitate to organisations which offer them autonomy and project-based work rather than slotting them into a hierarchical career.'[18]

One large London church completed a building project with much effort by a congregation containing a good proportion of Generation Xers. The leaders then appealed for resources so that it could be used for the Gospel, but failed to specify any further definitive project for that purpose. Money for that was much, much harder to realise.

Openness and teammates

It is easy to say that one of the values of Generation Xers is 'openness' and then move on to consider other things. Strategic leaders, however, stop here and pause. How can they build their team together? Different leaders will do this in various ways. One might take everyone to a show one evening, another invite everyone and their families to a barbecue or firework party, someone else will want to take them away for a day to relax, laugh and joke together.

Team building, however, is more than special events, key though these may be. It has to be seen in the day-by-day working, listening to what people are saying, and especially using them according to their gifts. This is particularly important since it implicitly shows that the leader knows them well enough to recognise what their gifts are, and that these gifts are appreciated and valued.

The same is true of successful churches. In one church, the youth group was not working as smoothly as it might. They had a discussion (openness) and 'realised we had all been trying to be good at everything'.[19] So they reassigned the various tasks so that the natural extrovert was the person who did the welcome and large group activities, the people-person was responsible for social activities, the detailed person prepared the Bible study materials, and so on. This rearrangement worked, with those involved looking forward to the weekly activity and enjoying taking their turn, because each person was now being used *according to his/her gifts*, one of the key traits of winning teams, as Belbin called them.

In his latest book, John Adair, an international leadership consultant, described the same thing in different words: 'Effective leadership is a relationship rooted in community.'[20] Gillian Stamp would see this as an outworking of the principle of subsidiarity, 'whatever each individual can do with his or her own power should not be done by the community'.[21]

Duncan Banks, leader of Banbury Community Church, puts it like this: 'The key to growing successful churches is growing successful leaders. The key to growing successful leaders is choosing *affinity* over ability [or even availability!]'[22] (my italics). Another salient phrase is to 'recognise the *authenticity* of persons'.[23]

There is a hidden implication in this process: if affinity is important, what might this particular group, so attached to each other, actually accomplish? In other words, what might be the God-given strategy for this group of people as they work together? The strategic leader will try and answer that question.

Some years ago a graduates' fellowship wanted to know the professionalisms represented by its members and found that 57% said 'teaching'. The leaders then asked the question, 'What would God have us do when we have in this group so many training skills?' (though they found they couldn't answer it!).

The same question can arise in a church: given this group of people, what is the best project they could collectively accomplish? However, while it may be a fair question, this is not likely to yield strategic leadership. Ultimately, that can only come through vision, which then is encapsulated in the project, and it is the project that draws supporters.

Courage

In the film *Braveheart* William Wallace stirs a hesitant Robert the Bruce by saying, 'Men don't follow titles, they follow courage.'[24] That is especially true of Generation Xers. Leadership has to be earned; it does not come by occupying a certain position. This is as true of Christian leadership in churches and charitable organisations as it is in commerce or business or education. 'People will follow you ... long-term only if they've learned to trust you.'[25]

Hezekiah had enormous courage in standing firm against the might of Nebuchadnezzar's armies around his city. He may be praised for his faith and trust in God, but the willingness to stand out in such a determined way was not easy (Is. 36:2,21). But his people stood with him because of his courage.

Daniel, too, was a man of increasing courage. Initially he just spoke to the chief of the eunuchs (Dan. 1:8), but later his companions faced the might of a furious emperor (3:18), and he himself told Nebuchadnezzar to 'break off your sins' (4:27). Towards the end of his life he continued to pray to God when he knew the punishment for doing so was to be thrown to the lions (6:10).

Moses also was a man of huge courage. He confronted Pharaoh not once, but many times, but that was almost as nothing compared to the fury of the Israelites in the wilderness against his leadership! He stood firm. The basic principle 'what you do today should lead to an outcome in the future'[26] was true for him. Like Luther, Moses would have said, 'I can do no other.'

What, then, is courage? Knowing yourself and knowing your God. Understanding the situation and appreciating its strategic importance. Being willing to risk all. Ultimately, however, it is not knowledge, but action. Doing something, often unexpected, but unflinchingly. Going forwards because you cannot go back without destroying what you stand for. It is being brave and bold and acting fearlessly, though the greatest courage is shown by the fearful who have to overcome their fear.

Doug Balfour, as Chief Executive, felt he should re-structure TearFund and redefine its essential purpose. The upheaval as the many options were evaluated almost undid the process, which took longer than expected. The out-turn, however, is a stronger, better organisation, which has been signally blessed by God in its work in recent years.[27]

David North, Managing Director of the publisher Pan Macmillan, speaking about his boss Les Higgins, said:

> The one thing he taught me was persistence in the face of adversity. There might be things you would give up on, because there were too many people within your organisation conspiring to make you fail, but if you really think it is the right thing to do, keep your eye on the goal and be robust about it.[28]

Courage means carrying through what you have begun, despite the opposition. It is being sure enough of one's vision to keep at it, despite whatever happens. Courage means a certain indifference to the names thrown at you, even the charges levied against you. It is trusting that righteousness will ultimately prevail, whether given by an earthly court, or recognised by the heavenly court.

Courage must not be equated with pig-headedness or inflexibility as it can also mean taking an alternative course of action when necessary. Courage is not blind. It seeks to listen, weigh up and respond appropriately, though often to a different set of values from those who think differently. Courage is ultimately about values.

All modes of strategic thinking require courage to be put into practice. Some may require more courage than others, but none will be successful without courage, shown in courageous, strategic, leadership in moving forwards. People follow courage, not position. Courage depends ultimately upon vision, and therefore wanting to win the game you are playing.

> Mind must be stronger, heart must be bolder,
> Courage must be greater, as our power grows less.[29]

Humility

It is not accidental that the greatest leader in the Old Testament, Moses, was also 'the most humble person in all the world' (Num. 12:3, CEV). Jesus too was similarly characterised: 'I am gentle and humble' (Mt. 11:29, CEV).

The word 'humble' is not used in the book of Daniel about himself, although he has the boldness publicly to accuse Belshazzar of not having humility (Dan. 5:22). He clearly tells Nebuchadnezzar that his (Daniel's) ability to interpret his dream came from God (2:28), and in his incredible prayer in chapter 9 identifies himself very clearly with sinful Israel (9:5, for example); both illustrations of humility.

It is less clear whether one would describe King Hezekiah as humble, though he asks Isaiah for advice (2 Kgs. 19:4), and begs the Lord to keep them safe (verse 19). These three leaders, discussed in Chapter 3, are either specifically stated to be humble or appear to be so by their actions.

Strategic leadership and humility go together. Many years ago Lord Longford wrote a book simply called *Humility*.[30] It seemed to me such a conflicting contrast that a peer could talk about humility that I bought the book, and in reading it came face to face with this extraordinary man's depth of spirit, which in later years was epitomised by the constant visiting of prisoners, even in his 90s, including such prisoners as the Moors' murderer Myra Hindley.

What is humility? Amongst other things, not taking the credit. Having a servant attitude. Knowing one's weaknesses. Knowing that good ideas (and vision) originate outside of ourselves. A Christian leader asked advice from his minister one day. He was wanting to do something which would, if successful, bring considerable prestige. Should he go ahead with it? 'Yes,' said the minister, 'your humility is strong enough to cope.' Wise words, and true in the fulfilment when the task was done and the prestige given. Some would say that recognising humility in oneself is the surest proof that it is completely lacking, but I am not sure that is true. You can *choose* to be humble.

Christian humility does NOT mean holding back, not taking a public position, or foregoing a strategic opportunity. Rather, having taken such actions, it is being sincerely able to give the glory to God. 'Not to us, O Lord, not to us, but to thy name give glory' (Ps. 115:1). This is not just a statement about humility, however, but also a motivation for service – our aim in all our strategic thinking, strategic leadership and vision building is to give glory to God.[31]

I once heard a Christian leader say, 'I hope I get appointed to such-and-such a job; that will be the crown of my career.' That does not appear a humble approach. On one occasion I asked a Diocesan Bishop if he were interested in a training course we were organising for Bishops. He replied, 'I think I can assume that those who appointed me to this job had sufficient confidence in my abilities to be able to do it without further education.' I have to confess to being slightly lacking in sympathy when a major leadership crisis occurred in his Diocese a few years later!

What, then, is humility? Ultimately service. The washing of a person's feet is a token of humility. It is being willing to spend time doing what is essential or even menial, but is unlikely to be noticed. It is undertaking the little, or the smelly, or the awkward, or the inconvenient thing. Not everyone who is humble is a leader; sadly not everyone who is a leader is humble.

Humility is also recognising the good in others, truly wanting *their* best, not serving their own interests, thanking the Lord for the privilege of being allowed to interact with them for a while along life's journey. It is the ability to see the greater, and to know oneself as truly a drop (but a very real drop) in a huge ocean.

In his book *Good to Great*,[32] Jim Collins examines over 1,400 companies in a research project entitled 'What catapults a company from being merely good to truly great?' Only 11 had made that jump. 'The most powerfully transformative executives' built enduring greatness by possessing 'a paradoxical mixture of personal humility and professional will', or 'fierce resolve', as he describes it.

Strategic leadership is nothing if we have no humility. If I 'have not love [which includes humility], I am a noisy gong or a clanging cymbal' (1 Cor. 13:1). An arrogant or self-important strategic leader appears to others as always blowing his/her own trumpet and 'sounding' off about his/her own ideas. He/she lacks one of the key characteristics likely to symbolise a successful ministry.

Humility is also being aware of one's personal abilities in relation to others, conscious that the talents one has are given, not learned. People are most productive when they build their lives around their strengths. Some would say that your talents are enduring and unique to you; you have the greatest room for growth in your areas of greatest strength,[33] but others that our areas of greatest weakness are the greatest areas of potential growth in the spiritual realm.

Vision

We have come full circle. This is a book about building vision, and thinking how that may be accomplished. It has also been a book about leadership, strategic leadership, which requires at its heart a clear vision. A former Bishop of Guildford, Rt Revd Michael Adie, once said that there were three types of clergy (and doubtless of any kind of leader): those who were obviously busy; those who were not obviously busy; and those who were obviously not busy.

The strap line was, however, all important. 'It is only the middle group', he said, 'who will have the time to fulfil their vision', or perhaps to think strategically.[34] This is very true.

Personal vision

There are, however, two visions. There is the personal vision and the corporate vision. If the first cannot be contained within the second, then it is time for the visionary to seek another job. If the first can be partially outworked through the second, then there is a strong commitment to it. The first, however, is probably broader than the second, and needs to be worked out over a longer time period.

The reason my colleague, Heather Wraight, works with me is that when I was looking for an Assistant Director I asked her the question, 'What is your personal vision?' Her answer was immediate and almost identical to my own: 'To help Christian leaders lead effectively.' There are many differences in our gifts, personalities and ways of working, but the common vision enables us to work together and overcome the differences.

Where there is no vision, the leader perishes, along with his/her people.

Vision, therefore, is the key component of strategic leadership. It provides the motivation, the energy, the *raison d'être*. We all have but one life; we pass this way but a single time. What do you wish to accomplish in it?

Vision is crucial

Vision assumes an ability to think forwards. Like strategic thinking, not everyone can. Government statisticians suggest that the high proportion of households in heavy financial debt is partly because of people's inability to plan forwards. Interestingly, the proportion *not* in debt is roughly the same as the proportion able to think strategically, about a third of the total.

Nick Page dwells on the same thought in his excellent book on postmodern values, *Blue*. He writes: 'Perhaps the proverb is true. Perhaps the elephant's memory is so strong that it becomes a kind of prison: because he knows what has always been, he is incapable of imagining what might be.'[35] William Blake summed it up admirably:

We are led to believe a lie
When we see with, not through, the eye.

Leadership without vision is not leadership in any strategic sense. It may involve many duties, and be a very busy position, but that does not equate to leadership. Leadership is knowing what you want to achieve and with the Lord's help seeking to work with others to achieve it. The word 'vision' is not essential in this process, but the concept behind the word is crucial. Objective, task, step, goal are all words that some use instead. Fine! There is, however, one further critical aspect – it needs to be articulated, preferably succinctly, in such a way that people will follow it and be enthused by it.

'Goals unattainable now', said the Polish philosopher Leszek Kolakowski, 'will never be reached unless they are articulated when they are still unattainable.'[36] The former Archbishop of Canterbury, George Carey, once said, 'Acknowledge the vision, grasp it and run with the opportunities.'[37]

Vision identified

Vision has to be articulated, and then ultimately personified. It is not the dead letter of the law, but the living life of the Spirit. It is that which will take us into tomorrow. Strategic leaders have such a vision, as this quotation from a Professor of Theology makes clear, and a 'passion for the cause' (in which the voluntary sector excels)[38] as well:

> The strategic leader is driven by a vision – a vision of the role that the institution can play in a changing world – and by a desire to share this vision with others.[39]

If a person is driven by a vision, he/she will be passionate about it. He/she will excite others when describing what he/she wants to do. Nothing was ever accomplished by a person without energy; part of that energy is in the articulation of the vision or message. John Wesley travelled on horseback the equivalent of ten times around the world's equator. He preached as often as 15 times a week for 50 years. He authored more publications in English until the science fiction writer Isaac Asimov came along. He read books while making his horseback journeys. When past 80, he complained he could not read and work more than 15 hours a day![40] John Wesley is an example of a passionate 'strategic leader driven by a vision'.

Ascertaining your vision may be helped by the following diagram:[41]

Figure 8.1
The missing piece

ISSUES	INSIGHT	INITIATIVES
Issues Needs Problems Challenges Opportunities	→ Deciding on what initiatives to take in response to what issues →	Activities Programmes Initiatives Projects Changes
RESOURCES RICH	**RESOURCES POOR**	**RESOURCES RICH**

The figure highlights the critical gap that lies between the problems and opportunities and the means of solving them. Identifying the problems and opportunities is not usually particularly difficult and there is plenty of help available from a wide range of sources. Likewise, there is a plethora of programmes and projects that *might* be the answer. Strategic leaders are able to provide the insight to know which way forward is likely to be the most effective in their context. So rather than trying this and that in the hope something will work, as many leaders actually do, they can present a clear vision of what they believe to be the way forward.

The vicar of one south London church[42] looked at the problems and decided that a new response the church could make was to start a midweek lunchtime outreach to workers in the area. This has now been started in a pub in the centre of town. It began from a careful exploration of the issues and deciding which initiative would be the best response.

Someone once said, 'If God entrusts a person with a new vision, the task ahead is never as great as the power that is behind.'

Not always successful

It is easy to assume that if one is 'playing to win' there is a good chance of winning: accomplishing one's objective. It is a reasonable assumption, but it doesn't always work out that way, and sometimes the strategic leader him/herself is the key reason why!

Relational difficulty

Strategic leaders, says researcher George Barna, are:

> those who analyse information, evaluate options and recommend the most effective courses of action. They are the strongest types of leaders when it comes to faith maturity and exhibiting Biblical wisdom. However, they are most prone to difficulties with their temper and their speech. They become so passionate about the paths they have discovered that they may lose patience with people who hold different opinions or who fail to understand why the path the strategic leader suggests makes the most sense.[43]

George Barna is not the only one to point out this failure to be people-people.[44]

Not always great

Strategic leaders may not like the implications, but many would say this statement is true of them: 'The greatness of an organisation will be directly proportional to the greatness of its leader.'[45] Sinclair Ferguson, a preacher, once said, 'the church can survive without great preachers; but she can't survive without good preachers'.[46] The suggestion is that the same is true of leaders. I suspect Jim Collins, however, would disagree and say they have to be both good *and* great. Part of the problem for the church is that, like his research which found only 11 out of over 1,400 companies had such leaders, this kind of quality leadership is comparatively rare, even amongst church leaders.

Being diverted before completion

Hitler's plan at the beginning of the Second World War was to sweep across the continent and then invade England. As England was an island, the German army would have to cross by ships, which he knew would be attacked by the Royal Air Force. So the Royal Air Force had to be defeated. One key way of doing that was to ensure that the British fighters did not know when the Germans were attacking, so the German Air Force Command ordered the bombing of all British radar stations.

This was almost completed when it was decided that a better tactic would be to bomb the actual airfields. This also proved a highly successful strategy, as the German bombers were able to bomb the airfields more quickly than they could be repaired.[47]

However, in the middle months of 1940, Churchill ordered British bombers to bomb a number of German cities, including Berlin. Hitler was so outraged that in retribution he ordered the bombing of London (what we now know as the Blitz). A key component of this occurred on 15th September 1940. That day (in what proved to be the finale of the Battle of Britain) 220 German aircraft set out to bomb London, defended by more than 400 fighters, but the Nazis lost 60 planes against 13 belonging to the Royal Air Force.

This loss made Hitler, two days later, on 17th September, suspend the plan to invade Britain. He decided to conquer Russia first instead. What was it then that went wrong with the German strategy? It was a good strategy, and the bulk of the thinking behind it was correct thinking. There were two key mistakes:

- Firstly, the Germans decided to change doing something successful *before it had been totally accomplished.* They switched from bombing the radar stations to bombing airfields, and then switched to bombing London instead of the airfields, without completing either.

- Secondly, a key reason for changing tactics (and therefore strategy) was because of the *anger of the senior leader.* Something had gone wrong, Berlin had been bombed. However, in terms of the overall war effort, so what? Hitler reacted to the local and tactical instead of taking the long-term view of the major and strategic. As a consequence he lost an opportunity that he was never able to regain.

This shows how the strategic leader needs to keep pressing on, despite setbacks. Completing each task is critical, however angry, annoyed or frustrated the strategic leader may be. Personal emotions must not be allowed to change strategic directions. Setbacks mean evaluating their importance and their level: are they at the strategic level or the operational or tactical level? The Military Model is important here. Tactical and even operational setbacks must not be allowed to sabotage the overall strategy.

Playing to win!

Who then, are strategic leaders? This chapter has suggested they are those with two main characteristics – an ability to *work with others* (understanding and knowing their intelligence, for example), and in the process adapting also to such other factors as experience, need or circumstance.

Secondly, such leaders *know themselves,* are humble about their abilities and gifts, but have the courage to follow their vision. Above all, strategic leaders are those whose vision is catching, exciting and wanted.

The old question was 'Are leaders born or made?' Strategic leaders are *both* born *and* made. They are born with inherent gifts but made through their experiences. Rosemary Aldis, former Personnel Director of OMF International, feels that creative and strategic thinking are gifts from God; we cannot grow them.[48] How do you spot strategic thinkers? Ask them what they would do if they were in charge![49]

There is something about strategic thinkers that sets them apart, a 'presence'. That something is fired in the furnace of life, which causes a deep, strong and enabling concern to develop. That in turn demands to be fulfilled – a vision. It might also be termed the ability to see the invisible, or the big picture.

Strategic leaders use strategic thinking, maybe a mix of all four types, but they do not stop there. They go further, which, borrowing from an old chorus, might be stated: They …

Dare to be Daniel! Or a Moses! Or a Hezekiah! Just dare!

Well, what are *you* waiting for? Don't you want to *play to win*? President Theodore Roosevelt once said, 'Do what you can, with what you have, where you are.'

Notes

[1] See, for example, Edward de Bono, *Six Thinking Hats: An Essential Guide to Clearer Thinking in Business Management* (Viking, Harmondsworth, Middlesex, 1985); Michael Robert, *Strategy Pure and Simple: How Winning CEOs Outthink their Competition* (McGraw-Hill, London, 1993); Michael Porter, *Competitive Strategy: Techniques for Analysing Industries and Competitors* (Free Press, MacMillan, New York, 1985); Philip Kotler and Alan Andreasen, *Strategic Marketing for Non Profit Organizations* (Englewood Cliffs, New Jersey: Prentice-Hall, 1987).

[2] Oswald Sanders, *Spiritual Leadership* (London: Marshall, Morgan & Scott, 1967), p. 19.

[3] Edward R. Dayton and Ted W. Engstrom, *Strategy for Leadership* (Old Tappan, New Jersey: Fleming H. Revell, 1979).

[4] This fourfold description of different approaches comes from Paul Sandham, a management consultant, in a session with the Board of Christian Research in August 2001.

[5] Charles Handy, *The Hungry Spirit* (London: Hutchinson, 1997), p. 211.

[6] In choosing the word 'Windows' for its product, Microsoft was absolutely spot on!

[7] Peter Schakel, '"Let the Pictures Tell their Own Moral": C.S. Lewis and Moral Imagination', *The Canadian C. S. Lewis Journal* No. 100 (Autumn 2001), p. 30.

[8] Supplement 'Mastering People Management' with the *Financial Times*, 12th November 2001, p. 6.

[9] R. Meredith Belbin, *Management Teams: Why they Succeed or Fail* (London: Butterworth-Heinemann, originally published in 1981).

[10] Interview with Sir Neil Cossons, Chairman of English Heritage, *Management Today*, 2001.

[11] George Barna, *A Fish out of Water* (Nashville: Integrity, 2002), p. 37.

[12] There are many different software tools available for the analysis of strategy. For example, there is gap analysis, share

analysis, the perceptual map, the Boston matrix, and so on. The Strategic Planning Society's magazine *Strategy* carries advertisements for such.

[13] Generational differences are explored in various books. See, for example, Peter Brierley, *Reaching and Keeping Tweenagers* (Christian Research, London, 2003), ch. 1 or Peter Brierley, *Turning the Tide: The Challenge Ahead – The Results of the 2002 Scottish Church Census* (Church of Scotland, Edinburgh and Christian Research, London, 2003), ch. 4.

[14] Richard Tiplady (ed.), *Postmission: World Mission by a Post-modern Generation* (Carlisle: Paternoster Press, 2002), p. 35.

[15] Ibid., pp. 36–7.

[16] George Barna, *Real Teens: A Contemporary Snapshot of Youth Culture* (Ventura, California: Regal, 2001), pp. 13–14.

[17] Barna, *A Fish out of Water*, p. 45.

[18] David Cannon, *Generation X and the New Work Ethic* (Demos, 1997) quoted in Revd Michael Moynagh and Richard Worsley, *Tomorrow's Workplace* (The Tomorrow Project, Nottingham, 2001), p. 36.

[19] Barna, *A Fish out of Water*, p. 98.

[20] Professor John Adair, *The Leadership of Jesus* (London: The Canterbury Press, 2001).

[21] Professor Gillian Stamp, 'Creative Church Leadership: But Me no Buts', a chapter to be included in a forthcoming book by MODEM, The Canterbury Press, London, distributed to participants at the Staff College, June 2003, p. 5.

[22] Duncan Banks, 'Where Rev Norman and Trev went Wrong', *Church Growth Digest*, Year 24, Issue 2, Winter 2002–03, p. 10.

[23] Revd Alan Strange, Norwich, *What do Church Leaders Think they are Doing?*, Windsor Project Essay for 2002 Course, ch. 3, p. 11.

[24] Barna, *A Fish out of Water*, p. 11.

[25] Gordon MacDonald, 'The Root of Leadership', *Leadership*, Winter 2003, p. 58.

[26] Ray McCauley preaching in Rhema Church, Johannesburg, South Africa, of which he is pastor, on Jeremiah 29:11, Sunday 1st July 2001.

27 Phil Iszatt and Andrew Boyd, *A Journey through Change: A Story of Organisational Transformation* (London: TearFund, 1999).

28 Danuta Kean, 'Macmillan's Man of the People', *The Bookseller*, 15th June 2001, p. 24.

29 The soldier Byrthwold, about to die in a battle in Maldon, Essex, in August 991, recorded in the Old English poem *Beowulf*.

30 Francis Aungier Pakenham, Earl of Longford, *Humility* (London: Fontana, Collins, 1970).

31 Cf. also Ron Preece, *Mainsprings for Action* (London: OMF, 1979), p. 9.

32 Jim Collins, *Good to Great* (HarperCollins, London, 2001), but taken from an article by Revd Arthur Siddall, 'Good to Great?', *MODEM Newsletter*, Issue 17, July 2001, p. 10.

33 Jill Garrett speaking at the CEO Forum arranged jointly by the Evangelical Alliance and Christian Research on 26th September 2000.

34 Rt Revd Michael Adie, Bishop of Guildford, speaking at the New Archdeacon's Conference in July 1996.

35 Nick Page, *Blue* (London: HarperCollins, 2001), p. 11.

36 Quoted in article by William A. Stahl, 'Technology and Myth', *Implicit Religion*, Vol. 5, No. 2, November 2002, p. 101.

37 Most Revd and Rt Hon George Carey speaking at the Oxford Diocesan Convention, as reported in the *Church Times*, 19th July 2002.

38 Jonathan Cormack and Mike Stanton, HayGroup and ACEVO, *Passionate Leadership: The Characteristics of Outstanding Leaders in the Voluntary Sector – What Sector Leaders Think* (London: Hay Group Management, 2003), p. 11.

39 Professor Robin Gill and Vice-Chancellor Derek Burke, *Strategic Church Leadership* (London: SPCK, 1996).

40 Example taken from John Haggai, *Lead On!* (Waco, Texas: Word, 1986), p. 136.

41 See note 4.

42 Christ Church, Bromley. The process was explained in a sermon by the vicar, Revd Iain Broomfield, on Sunday 8th September 2002.

[43] Barna, *A Fish out of Water*, and also e-mail from barnaup date@barna.org, 15th January 2003, p. 2.

[44] For example, Rosemary Aldis, in a private conversation, Singapore, 13th September 2001.

[45] Henry Blackaby. Barna, *A Fish out of Water*, p. xi.

[46] Editorial in *Themelios*, Vol. 26, No. 3, Summer 2001, p. 2.

[47] Based on the commentary of a 15-minute audio and visual presentation to mark the 60th anniversary of the Battle of Britain in the Royal Air Force Museum, Hendon, May 2002.

[48] Rosemary Aldis, private conversation (see note 44).

[49] Ibid.

About Christian Research

Christian Research began in 1993, but continued the aims of its predecessor, MARC Europe, which began ten years earlier in April 1983. Christian Research is an independent registered charity (Number 101 7701) and a company limited by guarantee (Number 279 2246). It is committed to:

- Collecting data about church and Christian agencies
- Interpreting the results and suggesting actions so that the Kingdom of God may grow
- Publishing resource volumes every two years like *Religious Trends* and the *UK Christian Handbook* (www.ukchristianhandbook.org.uk) (www.religioustrends.org.uk)

We serve all sections of the church in the Trinitarian group – Anglicans, Roman Catholics, Orthodox, Methodists, Baptists, United Reformed, and many smaller denominations. We do not do research for non-Trinitarian churches such as the Jehovah's Witnesses or Mormons.

We are particularly well known for our large-scale surveys of church attendance in the various countries of the United Kingdom, the most recent (before the 2002 Scottish Church Census) of which was the English Church Attendance Survey undertaken in 1998, whose results were published in the book *The Tide is Running Out*. Full details of our work may be seen on our web site:

www.christian-research.org.uk.

Other recent or forthcoming publications include:

- *101 Statistics that every Church Leader should Know* (April 2002)

- *Training Leaders to Think Strategically,* Major General Richard Dannatt (April 2002, Annual Leadership Lecture)

- Peter Brierley, *Reaching and Keeping Tweenagers* (January 2003, with workbook)

- Dr Andrew Sentance, *Successful Leadership in a Competitive Environment* (April 2003, Annual Leadership Lecture)

- Peter Brierley, *Turning the Tide: The Challenge Ahead*, Results of the 2002 Scottish Church Census (May 2003, with the Church of Scotland)

- *Religious Trends* No. 4 (2003/2004 edition, June 2003)

- *The Mind of Anglicans* (August 2003, with Cost of Conscience)

- *Leadership, Vision and Church Growth* (September 2003, results of a Salvation Army survey)

- Heather Wraight (ed.), *UK Christian Handbook* 2004/2005 edition (February 2004)

- Peter Brierley, *Conversations in a Pub: Understanding Church Statistics* (October 2004, with NexGen)

Christian Research has a Board of nine people. Its Chair in 2004 was Michael Smith, Managing Director of Lewis Springs, Birmingham. Christian Research is staffed by five full-time people (others help part time) and was started, and is currently headed, by Dr Peter Brierley as its Executive Director, a statistician with 36 years of experience with working on Christian evaluation, research and publishing.

Heather Wraight, who worked in communication for over 20 years, joined him in 1994 and is now Deputy Director.

For more information, either visit the web page given above, write to Vision Building, 4 Footscray Road, Eltham, London SE9 2TZ, phone 020 8294 1989, fax 020 8294 0014, or e-mail admin@christian-research.org.uk.

Alphabetical Index

Where a page number is followed by 'n' this refers to the note on that page; thus, for example, under Anderson, John '131n5' means Note 5 on Page 131.

Scripture Index

Where a page number is followed by 'n' this refers to the note on that page; thus, for example, under Anderson, John '131n5' means Note 5 on Page 131.